150 Creative Dates for a More Meaningful Marriage

150 Creative Dates for a More Meaningful Marriage

Nick & Mendy Greenwood

PLAIN SIGHT
PUBLISHING

An imprint of Cedar Fort, Inc.
Springville, Utah

ISBN 13: 978-1-4621-2243-1

Published by Plain Sight Publishing, an imprint of Cedar Fort, Inc.
2373 W. 700 S., Springville, UT 84663
Distributed by Cedar Fort, Inc., www.cedarfort.com

LIBRARY OF CONGRESS CATALOGING-IN-PUBLICATION DATA

Names: Greenwood, Mendy, 1968- author. | Greenwood, Nick, author.
Title: 150 creative dates for a more meaningful marriage / Mendy and Nick
   Greenwood.
Description: Springville, Utah : Plain Sight Publishing, an imprint of Cedar
   Fort, Inc., [2018]
Identifiers: LCCN 2018036727 (print) | LCCN 2018040194 (ebook) | ISBN
   9781462129287 (epub, pdf, mobi) | ISBN 9781462122431 (perfect bound :
   alk. paper)
Subjects: LCSH: Dating (Social customs)--Miscellanea. | Married
   people--Recreation.
Classification: LCC HQ801 (ebook) | LCC HQ801 .G69 2018 (print) | DDC
   306.73--dc23
LC record available at https://lccn.loc.gov/2018036727

Cover design by Shawnda T. Craig
Cover design © 2018 Cedar Fort, Inc.
Edited and typeset by Nicole Terry and Kaitlin Barwick

Printed in the United States of America

10 9 8 7 6 5 4 3 2 1

Printed on acid-free paper

For our girls: Erin, Shayna, McKenna, and Mallory.

It is our most earnest prayer that you will find in your future marriages what we have found in ours: love, laughter, commitment, trust, and enough memories to last for all eternity.

Love, Mom and Dad

CONTENTS

Dating 101 135

Tis the Season 147

About the Authors 163

OUTSIDE THE BOX

Some of your most meaningful and memorable times
together will take place when you just hold hands and jump.

1 WELL, THAT WAS RANDOM

For couples that like to live on the edge and be a little unpredictable, this is the
perfect way to spend an afternoon together. All it will take is a (paper) map of
your state or region, a blindfold, and a red marker to get you started. After that,
all you'll need is a full tank of gas and a big sense of adventure!

Start by unfolding the map and spreading it out on the floor or another flat
surface. One of you will put on the blindfold and stand in front of the map.
After your partner helps you spin around in place a couple of times (remember
Pin the Tail on the Donkey?), take the marker with the tip pointing straight
down and simply drop it onto the map. Wherever the marker lands and leaves
a dot is your date destination! If your marker drops very close to your home,
then take turns wearing the blindfold and choosing a random spot on the map.
More than one location will make the date even more interesting.

Depending on how far you will be traveling, pack a snack and some beverages. Definitely make a great playlist for the car ride and take a camera. Try to get as close as you can to the actual spot on the map, even if it's on the side of a country road, and snap a picture of the two of you at your destination! Sometimes the greatest discoveries come when you are off the beaten path, so soak in all the details, and you'll end up with a great "remember when" story!

2 MAKING HISTORY— FAMILY HISTORY!

Usually when a married couple spends time together, the conversation inevitably turns to their children, and sometimes that's perfectly okay. But for this date, try turning your heart and your conversation in the other direction. Looking back and discussing those who came before you might bring a spirit of closeness into your marriage that you were not expecting!

Getting Started

A pedigree chart (or family tree chart) has blanks laid out in a format to help you chart your family by generations. You start with yourself, and then add your parents, grandparents, great-grandparents, and so on. Usually one chart has about four generations represented on it. Print one out for you and one for your spouse.

You start simply with what you know. Most of us know our parents' full names (including maiden names) and what city and county they were born in. Do you know their birth dates? The year? What about their death dates and locations, if they have already passed away? This is all important information to have if you plan to continue to research your ancestors.

A lot of us know our grandparents' names, at least on one side—either maternal or paternal. But when we get past the second generation, things start to get a little fuzzy. We are talking about people you may have little or no memory of. This is where you might need some extra help.

Where do you turn now? According to *Family Tree Magazine*, these are three of the best websites to use when searching for genealogical records (there are many to choose from!):

- ancestry.com (small fee)
- archives.com (small fee)
- FamilySearch.org (free)

If you don't know the names of your grandmother's parents, for example, you can plug your grandmother's name in (along with all the other information you have, such as where she was born, died, or got married) and start searching records that have been compiled by experts from all over the world! When you discover her name on a census record or a birth certificate, you'll also find her parents' names.

Sometimes, if you are lucky, you'll also find some more information. You might find records of your great-grandfather's employment or military service. You might gain insight into what your great-grandparents' daily life was like when you find a newspaper clipping or a census record with the whole family listed. Did you know that your great-grandmother had six siblings? And that they lived in a two-bedroom house on a farm? Did you know that one of her brothers died from tuberculosis when he was three years old? You can stumble across all of this information and more with just a couple of hours of research. And now, instead of just names on a paper, you have a snapshot of their lives. Who knows—you may even find an actual snapshot of Great-Great-Grandpa Joe!

However, you must be warned! When you open this door to the past, be prepared! Family history research can be addicting! You will develop a love and closeness to the family members that you learn about as they become more familiar to you. Doing this research together with your soulmate will bring you even closer to them as you share memories and stories and become investigator-historians together.

This date will very likely turn into another and another and another as you dig deeper into the stories of your past.

3 That's Puzzling!

This might sound like an evening for Grandma, but some of the best conversations happen while sharing an activity that doesn't require much thinking. This date provides a great opportunity to build something together while having a much-needed heart-to-heart.

Start with the Invitation

Most craft stores sell small, blank puzzles that can be written or drawn on and then taken apart and put back together. Create an invitation to a "puzzle night," complete with the time and location for your date (even if it's at the dining room table!). Break the puzzle up and slip it in an envelope with your partner's name on it. Leave it in a place where he or she will find it a couple of days ahead of time.

Shop for the Perfect Puzzle

There are literally thousands of puzzles out there in nearly any price range. So how do you find the right one for your date? Consider the following:

- Are you hoping to finish it in one night, or will you leave it out and come back to it often? The more pieces, the longer it will take to complete. Be sure and check the number of pieces in the completed puzzle as you are considering how much time you want to invest.
- Is there a subject matter or theme that you are both interested in? There are puzzles based on TV shows, movies, historical places and people, animals, art, and so on. Does your spouse love cats? Cars? Flowers?

- Where are you going to be working on this puzzle? Check the finished size, and be sure you have a space large enough to hold the whole thing easily.

One more thought to keep in mind—what are you going to do with the puzzle when it is finished? Will you just pull it apart and put it back in the box? Or do you want to preserve your work of art? If you want to hold on to your finished work, be sure to investigate how you plan to preserve it with a search online. There are many techniques, widely ranging in cost.

Are You Ready to Get Started?

You'll want to eat before your start, and keep drinks on a different table. An accidental spill could destroy your hard work and your evening!

Now, put on some background music and get started early—puzzling can be addicting, and you may have a hard time calling it quits!

4 You Read My Mind!

A bookstore is a wonderful place to spend some time learning about each other and other interesting topics. You could easily spend a couple of hours just browsing different sections. A lot of bookstores have a cafe or coffee shop, which provides the perfect location to sit and talk afterward.

Here are some suggestions for how to make this date a meaningful and entertaining one:

- Children's section—Look for your favorite books from childhood, and read them to each other.
- Biography section—Find people that you either admire or dislike, and discuss why.
- Motivational or self-help section—Read affirming and uplifting quotes to each other.
- Humor section—Find a great joke book, and take turns reading your favorites.
- Cooking section—Look through recipes to spark your own cooking creativity. Decide on something new to try.
- Magazine section—Take a silly quiz together.
- Business section—Dream together about a small business you'd like to start one day.

Don't forget to have some browsing time. Ask each other to complete the sentence, "If I could have any book in this store it would be _____." Who knows—maybe you'll stumble upon a great gift idea for the next holiday or birthday!

"The love of learning, the sequestered nooks,
and the sweet serenity of books."
—Henry Wadsworth Longfellow

5 Page-Turner

Whether you are a Shakespeare fan or Harry Potter is more your style, curling up on the sofa or in bed and reading a book to each other can be an experience that you will return to again and again. As the story unfolds, you may start speculating together about what will happen next. You can come to know the characters and discuss them together, even choosing favorite heroes and villains. You may even start to spot symbolism to discuss . . . and what will happen next?

Make it a little more fun by choosing characters to read and using different voices to distinguish them.

Choose a book that you'd like to start reading together and designate some of your date nights to hide away and have your own private book club.

And the plot thickens . . .

6 WE'RE A MODEL COUPLE

When was the last time you had professional photos taken of you and your spouse—without the kids? Photo sessions are no longer limited to posed studio shots with hot lights and wearing your Sunday best. The process of capturing memories in photos is memorable in itself!

Do a little research in your area for specific pricing and terms, and don't forget to ask around for referrals. Photographers specialize in different types of images—some natural and candid, some traditional, and some artistic. Locations can vary too. You may take photos outside or inside, with a favorite pet or with a musical instrument. You may be in the studio or at home. Find a photographer who will capture not only your faces but also your relationship. This is what you hope to preserve through time, not the cute outfit you chose to wear or how your hair looked.

What to Expect

Most photographers will charge a "sitting fee." Depending on where you are in the country, this fee could be anywhere from $75 to $300 and should include the following:

- A pre-session consultation about the style you are looking for and for planning your location and your outfits (yes, more than one!)
- About two hours for the actual photo shoot (including outfit changes)
- A reveal session to look though the proofs and order digital images or prints (these cost extra)

Some photographers will even offer hair and makeup assistance on the day of the shoot!

Just keep in mind that one day your children will want photos to remind them of your love for each other, your laughter, and your devotion to one another. These images will become priceless to them. Take the time to capture these emotions in photos now, while you can. And why not make it a date and have a little fun with it?

7 Undercover Dinner Date

Tonight's dinner date is going to be a little different that your usual night out. Are you willing to allow your spouse to purchase your outfit for dinner? What if you only had to invest $10 and you had one hour to pick it out? This light-hearted date will have you laughing for years to come!

Let the Shopping Begin!

If your sweetie doesn't know your sizes, now is the time to come clean! Find a great thrift store near you and plan to arrive an hour or so before dinnertime. The idea is to find an outfit for your spouse to wear to dinner—the cheesier the better—for under $10 each and in under an hour!

Mismatched? Okay! Too big? Fine! Too small? Well . . . maybe not okay. Out of date? No problem! Just plain ugly? Yes!

Once your hour of shopping time is up and you have lovingly (laughingly) picked clothes for your spouse, go ahead to the dressing room, where you will change into your spiffy (not) new (sort of) attire and head out to dinner.

Time to Go Undercover!

When you walk out of the thrift store, you both agree to act like nothing has happened. You are wearing a plaid jumper from the 1980s . . . so what? Act as if you dress like this every day. Your outfit has more colors than a rainbow? Pretend as if you don't even notice.

In the car on the way to dinner (when you can stop laughing), you should make up new names for each other. Try to make it fit the "look" of the outfit you have been blessed (stuck) with. When you enter the restaurant, be sure to call each other by your "new" names. As a matter of fact, for the rest of the night, you play the part of these new characters.

Yes, you might get a few side-eyes and snickers, but deep down they wish they knew how to have fun like the two of you!

Be sure to document your date on social media, and feel free to donate the clothes back to the thrift store after you take them home and wash them.

8 My Favorite Things . . .

This date is all about putting your spouse first. Think of it as a gift. "Tonight, dear, we are going to do all of your favorite things." This would be an especially thoughtful way to cheer your spouse up if he or she has gone through a difficult time recently.

You can begin the week by leaving your sweetheart a note. Of course, you can add your own words, but you might start with something like this:

Dear _____ (your sweetie),

   "When the dog bites, when the bee stings, when I'm feeling sad.
   I simply remember my favorite things, and then I don't feel so bad!"

   I know you've had a hard time _____ (at work, at home, with the
kids, with your family, etc.) *lately, so I'd like to take you out on Friday night
to experience a few of your favorite things. Just to make sure I get it right, please
take some time this week to fill out the following suggestions:*

- *I've been craving:* _____ (restaurant)
- *I've been dying to see:* _____ (movie or play)
- *I think it would be fun to:* _____ (activity)
- *I have been wanting to listen to:* _____ (music)
- *I would feel refreshed if I had a:* _____ (foot rub, back
  massage, manicure, pedicure, facial, etc.)

Signed,
Your favorite ("guy" or "girl")

The rest is easy! Just try to get the note back at least a day before your
scheduled date so you can make arrangements to fulfill your date's favorite
things. You may not have time to do everything on one date, but this date will
remind your sweetheart that he or she is your number-one priority!

9 MORE THAN WORDS

In the best of marriages, a spouse is able to understand everything his or her
partner says—even if there are no words. How well do you hear the unspoken
communication that takes place within your relationship? On this date, you
will have your mouth closed and possibly your eyes opened.

Why is this important? Studies[1] have shown that couples with young children only talk to each other for ten minutes during an hour-long meal, while couples who have been married for thirty years only talk to each other for sixteen minutes during an hour-long dinner. Married couples that make it to the fifty-year mark are lucky to have more than a three-minute conversation during an hour of dinnertime. So if we aren't talking to each other, we'd better learn other ways to communicate!

1. "Why Silence Is Golden after a Happy Marriage: Couples Only Speak for 3 Minutes at Dinner," *Daily Mail*, April 9, 2010, http://www.dailymail.co.uk/femail/article-1264868/Why-silence-golden-happy -marriage-Couples-speak-3-minutes-dinner.html.

Games to Get You Started

1. Write down at least ten emotions together on slips of paper (e.g., surprised, disappointed, excited, afraid, devastated). Be creative! Take turns drawing them from a basket, and *using only your facial expressions* (no hand gestures), act out the emotion on the paper while your partner tries to name the emotion. Allow only about a minute per guess. See how well you can pay attention and read your partner's emotions.

2. Flip a coin to decide which one of you will be "heads" and which one will be "tails." Whoever is "heads" will be allowed to speak, and whoever is "tails" will have to find another way to communicate *without words* in the following scenario. This will help you understand how easy it is to be misunderstood if you don't communicate well.

> **Heads:** *Do you know where my keys are? I can't find them!*
> **Tails:** *Which keys? To which car?*
> **Heads:** *The minivan!*
> **Tails:** *Oh. No, I haven't seen them.*
> **Heads:** *What do you mean you haven't seen them? Didn't you drive the minivan last?*
> **Tails:** *Um . . . I don't think so. I think you did.*
> **Heads:** *Oh, right. I did. Sorry about that.*
> **Tails:** *No problem.*
> **Heads:** *But I still need to find my keys. I'm going to be late!*
> **Tails:** *Did you look in your coat pocket?*
> **Heads:** *Of course! That's the first place I looked!*
> **Tails:** *What about in the car?*
> **Heads:** *I don't ever leave my keys in the car!*
> **Tails:** *Really? Maybe you should check to be sure.*
> **Heads:** *Okay, if it will make you happy.*
> **Tails:** *It will.*

Heads: *I'll be right back. I'm going to check the car.*
Tails: *Wait! I found them . . . in my pocket.*

3. After dinner, when the dishes have been cleared, reach across the table and hold hands. You are going to stare into each other's eyes for three-minute increments—with *no words.* (Get out a timer!)

4. For the first three minutes, looking into the eyes of your sweetie, go back in time and remember the first time you saw him or her. What was he or she wearing? What was he or she doing? What did he or she say to you? What did you think of him or her at first?

5. For the second three minutes, think of a time you were proud of your husband or wife. Was it after a child was born? Was it a graduation? Was it an accomplishment at work? Was it the way he or she handled a difficult situation?

6. For the third and last three-minute increment, imagine the future. Where do you want to spend time together when you are retired and all the kids are gone? How do you imagine your home? How do you plan to show kindness and love to your spouse after fifty years of marriage?

7. Now that you've spend nine minutes staring into each other's eyes, you can spend the next full minute on a kiss!

8. Last but not least, wrap up your silent date with a silent movie! Netflix, Hulu, and even YouTube will have fun offerings in the silent movie category. So enjoy some popcorn, and finish your fun evening together with a little more silence.

"Silence is one of the great arts of conversation."
—*Marcus Tulles Cicero*

10 Lobby for Your Hobby

Do you have a hobby that you are passionate about but that you usually do without your spouse? Have you ever wished that your sweetie could better understand why it's so important to you? It might be time for you to lobby for your hobby!

One of the top ten reasons couples divorce is that they develop a general lack of interest in each other's lives. We often hear a couple "lost touch with each other" or "fell out of love." While "me time" is important and no two people are going to have identical passions all the time, it is vitally important for the two of you to stay connected to one another. Although you may never develop your husband's passion for fishing or golf, it is important to know and understand why he loves it so much. You may never love scrapbooking or shopping the way your wife does, but you need to understand what she gets out of it and what makes it so satisfying for her. And yes, you need to hold on to your individual identities and it is perfectly okay to enjoy activities without your spouse, but there should never be a part of your life that's completely closed off to him or her.

So how does this date work? It's simple. When (not *if*!) your husband invites you to that sporting event that he wouldn't miss if his life depended on it, consider yourself honored to be included in his passion and enthusiastically accept the invitation! When (not *if*!) your wife includes you in that charity event or a night of scrapbooking, soak up the opportunity to see her in her element.

Try very hard to see the date through the other's eyes, and allow yourself to love your spouse even if you don't love his or her hobby. Be passionate about your hobby, but be more passionate about your marriage!

11 Pick Three!

So it's date night and you haven't had a chance to plan anything? Are you tempted to catch up on your social media accounts while your sweetheart passes out on the couch? No way! Even date nights need a back-up emergency plan! To start with, we have to eliminate the following conversation:

> **Husband:** *"Where do you want to go for dinner?"*
> **Wife:** *"I don't know. Doesn't really matter to me."*
> **Husband:** *"How about burgers?"*
> **Wife:** *"Eh. Not really in the mood for burgers. Anything but burgers."*
> **Husband:** *"What movie do you want to see?"*
> **Wife:** *"I don't know. Doesn't really matter to me."*
> **Husband:** *"What about a thriller?'*
> **Wife:** *"Nah. Not a thriller. Not really in the mood for a thriller."*

So often couples scrap the idea of a date night because they haven't planned ahead and can't agree on what to do with their time together. For times like these, you can pull out the "pick three" jars and your no-hassle, easygoing date is planned in a few minutes.

- **Jar #1** contains small, folded pieces of paper with your favorite easy dinner ideas written on them. These can include carry-out meals, sandwiches made at home, or restaurants. Use restaurants that are in a reasonable price range so you can feel comfortable with your choice whether the bank account is fluffy or flat at the time.
- **Jar #2** contains activities that don't require a lot of advance preparation or decision-making and that you both usually enjoy. They can be a simple as watching a silly game show, reading a book together, playing a video game, or sitting quietly on the front porch.
- **Jar #3** contains dessert or snack ideas (e.g., popcorn, ice cream, cookies, crackers, etc.). If you have to make a quick run to the grocery store for this one, go ahead and take care of that before you start your date.

Make a silly ceremony out of pulling ideas from the "pick three" jars, complete with a drumroll, please. Now your biggest decision to make is who will be the one to pick. (Hint: You can take turns!)

Since these jars will likely be out in the public eye, you should try to make them somewhat attractive by decorating them. Keep them in a safe place for when you need them next!

12 First Time for Everything

As the years pass and life gets busier, we sometimes forget some of those important "firsts" that we shared together. Maybe you are still having "firsts," or maybe you are on your "fifths" of everything, but this date will take you back in time to talk and laugh about all those things that you did for the first time together.

Use this list to get started, but feel free to add more as you think of them. Just remember that this is not a time to bring up old wounds! Write these ideas on separate slips of paper and put them in a basket. Take turns reading one and telling everything you remember about that "first."

- First time you laid eyes on each other
- First time you kissed
- First meal you ate together
- First movie you saw together
- First car you had together
- First song you danced to at your wedding
- First time you met the in-laws
- First place you lived together
- First time you talked about marriage
- First time you said, "I love you"
- First argument
- First date
- First concert or show together
- First anniversary
- First pet together
- First vacation together
- First time you held hands in pubic
- First Christmas together

13 ESCAPE . . . WITH A PERSONAL AD

This is a fun combination of "Escape (The Piña Colada Song)" by Rupert Holmes and Mad Libs, and it can used to create (at least) two dates. Each of you fills in the blanks below with your own words and passes the completed song lyrics to the other. Then your job is to create the date that your spouse described! Put some thought and creativity into your answers and the date you plan for your loved one. Try to come up with ideas that your spouse may not think of and interests that they may not know you have.

If you like _____ (favorite dessert) *and getting caught in* _____ (climate/weather),

If you're not into _____ (something trendy), *if you have* _____ (good personal trait),

If you like _____ (activity) *at* _____ (time of day), *in the* _____ (location),

I'm the love that you've looked for. Come with me, and escape."

(Rupert Holmes, "Escape [The Piña Colada Song]," 1979.)

14 SURPRISE DAY OFF!

What would you do if you woke up on a Thursday with the sun shining, the birds chirping, and your sweetheart snoring beside you? You'd probably bolt out of bed in a panic and scream, "Get up, get up! The alarm didn't go off!" Well, just calm down—this is the perfect surprise date! If your spouse has been wishing for a little more time together, why not oblige? Especially on a birthday, anniversary, or any day that you'd just prefer to hang out together.

Just take a vacation day and (*shh!*) don't tell him or her. Wait until he or she has that moment of full-blown panic when the "alarm didn't go off" and very calmly say, "Oh, I took the day off. Surprise!"

What Now?

- Snuggle back in bed and go back to sleep for a while!
- Eat breakfast in bed
- Read the paper in bed
- Watch movies in bed
- Take silly magazine quizzes in bed
- Do a crossword puzzle together in bed
- Read a book together in bed

Do you get the picture? So maybe lying around all day isn't your idea of a date, but planning ahead and surprising your sweetie makes all the difference in the world. And sometimes we just need to close the blinds, fluff the pillows, stay in our PJs all day and spend a little no-fuss time together.

ROMANCE DOESN'T HAVE TO BE COMPLICATED

Sometimes our busy lives can cause us to be starved for romance but also short on energy, time, or money. Romance doesn't have to be complicated. Just let your loved one know how much he or she means to you with one of these suggestions.

15 OUR FAVORITE ROMANTIC MOVIE

Snuggle the couch together and watch your wedding video. If you can't get enough of the wedding, pull out the wedding photos. Recall all the funny moments from that amazing day, and take special time to tell your sweetie why you'd do it all again, in a heartbeat.

16 Our Town Is a Very, Very, Very Fine Place

If you had to sell your city or town to the public, could you do it? What do you love about your neck of the woods? Well, get out your smart phone or your handheld video camera because we've got a job for you!

Imagine you are a public relations team and you have been tasked with promoting your town. You have to make a video to present to "the investors" that will showcase why your town is the best place to be.

Have a creative brainstorming session. What kind of look and feel do you want your video to have? Hard-hitting, artistic, or more casual and conversational?

Decide where you need to capture your footage by going over the following questions (and any other ones you come up with):

- What do you love about where you live?
- Where do you like to eat?
- What's the best market in town or the best area for shopping?
- Where do you go to do the best people-watching, and what is your favorite local attraction?
- Is your town or city historically significant?
- What makes it unique?
- Who are the hometown heroes?
- What are the favorite sports teams?

Make it feel real. Include others in your video. For example, if your are recording a video of your favorite restaurant, get some footage with customers, wait staff, and possibly the owner talking about their food, atmosphere, and service.

Spend a few hours running all over town to film your favorites, and then if you have any video-editing software (most computers come with a simple editing program), splice your segments together and add voice-overs and background music.

When you are done, post your video on social media with the title "What We Love about Our Town," and get others to post their own comments, photos, and videos. If your comments are positive and the video gets good attention, shoot it off to the local news station or the city manager. Who knows—your video (and your date night) may become part of a whole new promotion for your town!

17 YARD SALE

Everybody's favorite time of year is yard-sale season, right? Some might disagree and claim it to be Christmas, but for those of us who love unique items at a bargain price, yard-sale season *is* like Christmas! So push or pull your sweetheart out of bed before the sun comes up because items for sale scattered all over the city are calling your name, and somebody else might be buying them! This early morning date will be an adventure.

Make it meaningful. Think of something specific that you are "hunting" for, and make it a team effort. Maybe a specific tool, a piece of furniture, or an appliance.

Make it funny. After looking over someone's yard sale merchandise, make up a secret identity for him or her (think: spy) based on the items that your saw for sale.

Make it "green." Search for something that you can refinish, update, or upcycle, and make it a project you work on together.

Even if you don't find anything you'd like to take home, the morning has still been productive! You started your day early, spent a few hours with your sweetie, and met a few of your neighbors. Until next week!

18 ESTATE SALE

Estate sales have a certain mystique and mystery about them, and they can be a very romantic way to spend an afternoon with your loved one. You may find a treasure, or you may not find anything of monetary value, but at the very least you will have a day filled with possibilities!

Important Tips

- Go on the first day of the sale before the estate has been picked over, and get in line early. The sellers might limit the number of people that are allowed to walk through the house at a time, and you want to get the first look!
- Take cash in your pocket, but don't take a huge bag. You probably won't be allowed to take it in.
- Don't feel uneasy about wandering through the house, including areas that are typically private, such as bathrooms, basements, and closets. If a room or door is off limits, organizers will mark it with a sign. Don't be afraid to ask questions of the organizers if you are curious about a particular piece—even if it does not appear to have a price tag.

What to Look For

- Jewelry
- Old books
- Furniture (no upholstery)
- Silverware, glassware, and dishes

What to Ignore

- Large appliances
- Cookware
- Upholstered furniture (may have bed bugs or odors that are difficult to remove)

It makes the day even more interesting if you remember that this is (or was) somebody's home—not just a showroom floor. These items are personal, and they have a story. If you are lucky enough to walk away with a piece of jewelry (even if it's costume jewelry) or a book that has handwriting in it, you will be taking a piece of history with you. Now that is true romance!

19 CATCHING UP

Everybody has times when the laundry gets out of control and it takes forever to catch up. Sometimes our relationships get neglected and need some catching up as well. This wonderful date idea takes care of both!

Spend some time gathering all of your dirty laundry together, *all* of it. Don't forget the sheets and the towels! If it's *really* behind, you may have to pull out a couple of suitcases and pack them as well. Grab your laundry detergent, dryer sheets, fabric softener, and whatever else you typically use to get that laundry clean and fresh. Also, take a lot of quarters. Most washers at a laundromat will charge you $3–$4 per load, and the dryers will give you about ten minutes for every quarter. Thankfully they are very large capacity and can hold more than your machines at home.

Laundry is typically done in four stages, as we are all aware: washing, drying, fluffing and folding, and putting it all away. Your date night will have those four stages as well!

Stage 1: The WASHING Stage (approximately 45 minutes)

Sort your clothes as you normally would—lights and darks, delicates and heavy duty—then fill up those washing machines and let the cleaning begin.

While your clothes are in the washing machines, talk to each other. Clean up some things. Sort out your "dirty laundry."

- **Lights and delicates:** Are there some plans you need to make? Some loose ends you need to tie up?

- **Dark and heavy duty:** Is there a decision that you've been putting off? Is there an apology you need to make? Is there an issue that needs to be addressed?

Take this washing time to tie up some things that need to be addressed with a strict understanding that as soon as the buzzer goes off, you are going to move on to the next stage—with no lingering stains or dirt!

Stage 2: The DRYING Stage (approximately 45 minutes)

Throw your wet clothes into the dryers, toss in some dryer sheets to cut down on the static electricity, and put in a few quarters. When you press the start button, the drying stage begins!

While the dryers are warming up your clothes, spend some time "warming up" to each other. Hold hands, snuggle close, and pull out some snacks.

Now is the time to share some warmth with your spouse:

- "Thank you for putting the kids to bed last night when I was so exhausted."
- "I'm really proud of you for how hard you worked to make the yard look nice."
- "I notice that you always send the kids out the door in the morning with a hug and a positive word. You are a great mom."
- "You are such a kind and thoughtful person—I'm so glad I chose to marry you!"

Breathe some air back in to your relationship with some kind words. You will be amazed at how a simple "thank you" can warm things up after a long week. But don't rush it! Use the entire drying time, and don't be afraid of some quiet moments. Just stay close and enjoy the warmth!

Stage 3: The FLUFFING AND FOLDING Stage

So now the laundry is all clean, it smells nice, it's wrinkle-free, and it's and warm. This is the best part! Start pulling out the clothes folding them. (Don't forget to keep the dryer tumbling so nothing gets wrinkled.)

The fluffing and folding stage is the time to get silly! Keep it warm, tell funny stories, joke around, and laugh at each other. Have fun together.

Sage 4: The PUTTING IT ALL AWAY Stage

What a relief to have all that laundry caught up and put away. Sometimes we don't even realize how far we have fallen behind until we catch it all up again.

Isn't it the same with our relationships? They feel so much better when they are clean, warm, wrinkle free, and folded neatly so that we can find them when we need them.

20 Open-House Hunting

Are the two of you dreaming about a new house or a home-improvement project? Why not spend an afternoon checking out the homes in your city or town? You'll be inspired with new ideas for your own home by what you see in other's houses. The best way to do it (and the legal way!) is through the "open house" listings in your community.

If you do an internet search for "open houses in [your city]," you'll find a list (and probably a map) with locations and times of upcoming open house opportunities. You can use well-known sites such as Zillow and Trulia, or you could check out the page of a local real estate agency. After that, make a plan so you don't spend your time crisscrossing through town. Also, be sure to bring a notebook or a journal so you can make notes about your new ideas when you get back in the car.

If you just can't get enough of seeing the inside of other people's homes and you want to take this date one step further, watch for when your city or town has a "parade of homes" or a "tour of homes." These annual tours attract a wide audience from design idea hunters to mild house hunters to the serious new home buyers. These are usually executive showcase homes decorated with the hottest design trends and newest construction models. Sometimes the tour is free, self-guided, and open to the public, and other showcase home tours benefit a local charity and therefore charge a fee. Nonetheless, these homes will definitely leave you inspired and ready to make some "dream home" changes of your own.

What a fun and inspiring way to spend an afternoon together!

> *"Mid pleasures and palaces though we may roam,*
> *Be it ever so humble, there's no place like home."*
>
> —*John Howard Payne*

21 Living Room Lair

Remember building a living room fort when you were young? I remember building one every chance I had. Unfortunately, I was limited by the few resources at my disposal. Now, as an adult, those resources have expanded—and not just because of a larger budget, more access to better materials, or the fact that I don't have to worry about dismantling everything before my parents get home. I'm more mature now, and that means that my imagination, planning skills, and creativity have matured as well. And the fact that I give myself permission to make a fort is liberating.

This date will be sure to transport you and your spouse to a more magical time when a castle or cavern could be manufactured from bed sheets and blankets. Here are a few logistical lists to consider if you want to take your living room lair to the next level!

What You'll Need

- Binder clips—Clips instead of pins are easier to see when it's finally time to take everything down. And you won't have to worry about being pricked by tiny, hard-to-see pins.
- String—Consider using strings of different thicknesses. Heavier string can be used for draping sheets and blankets over while thinner string can be used to tie sheet corners to hooks.
- Command hooks—These temporary hooks are a great resource for hanging sheets from walls, furniture, and even the ceiling. When it's time to take everything down, they won't leave marks or holes.

- Lamps—Be sure to have the proper lighting for you and your spouse to read, for watching a movie or TV show, or for talking.

Obligatory Safety Concerns

- No open flames—It should be common sense that any open flames (whether they are from a fireplace, wood-burning stove, or candles) and sheets/blankets don't play well together. Use another source for light: lamps, flashlights, glow sticks scattered throughout, and so on.
- Heavy objects—Don't use your ceramic cat statue to anchor a sheet on the edge of a console stereo. Heavy objects can easily be pulled down onto someone who may be crawling past.

Design Considerations

- Size/rooms—Design your fort based on the size of the room you're in or the requirements of your date activity. If you and your spouse just want a cozy space to sit and talk or read together, make it smaller. If you would like to be able to stretch out and watch a movie, be sure the room you're in can accommodate that.
- Comfort areas—Depending on the size, you can set up some fluffy pillows, chairs, area rugs, and/or tables. Whatever you end up with, be sure to make it comfortable by staying away from anything course or scratchy. You don't want your date to end earlier than it should due to discomfort that could be avoided.
- Entertainment—Try to incorporate a TV into your lair. If that's not possible, set up a laptop or tablet to make it easy to view a movie or TV show. You could also just listen to a playlist that's meaningful to the both of you.

Building a fort is a whimsical, childlike thing to do, but it's a great opportunity for you and your spouse to relax and be silly together. You won't be just constructing a fort; you will also be creating blissful memories!

22 Flea Marketing

Every state has flea markets and swap meets, and this is one of our favorite dates! It only has to cost what you want it to cost, and you will find interesting and memorable items (and people) every single time you go!

Make It More than Just Browsing

Of course, we all could keep ourselves occupied for hours just walking aimlessly through a flea market, table to table, vendor to vendor, picking up and putting down items that catch our eye. But remember, this is a *date*, so here are some ideas about how to make it feel like one.

Have a treasure hunt. Set a spending limit—whatever your budget allows. Nothing is too small at a flea market! Pick a room in your house and shop together for a "treasure" for that room within your spending limit. Along the way, you'll have a great time talking about interesting items or meeting quirky vendors.

Make it competitive. What is your favorite movie to watch together? With $5 each and a fifteen-minute time limit, set out to find the most creative and unique item that ties to that movie. Have a meeting spot designated to share your finds at the end of your time limit.

Do it again with your favorite vacation spot in mind, or your favorite holiday or favorite color. You can change the time limit or spending limit at any time!

Make it sentimental. Again, decide on a spending limit and a time frame to work within. Set out to find your spouse the most meaningful gift you can in that time frame and budget. Come back together, and present your treasures over a hot dog and some nachos (the universal flea market meal). Who knew a day at the flea market could be so romantic? (We did!)

23 First Date, Again

For some reason, no matter how long we've been married, that first date is something we always remember. Over the years, those details might become a little fuzzy or a little romanticized, but we never forget where we went, how we got there, and all the embarrassing things we think we did wrong.

So what if we could relive that first night out together? Some of the details might be impossible to recreate, especially if a lot of time has passed or if you have moved away. But the important thing is to "meet" your spouse all over again.

- Did your guy show up at the door wearing a suit, bearing a bouquet of flowers?
- Did you go to an Italian restaurant or McDonald's?
- Did you go to a movie or play miniature golf? Did you just go for a walk?
- What did you talk about over dinner? It's unlikely that you talked about the kids or the bills!

Do the best you can to recreate the first date you had together. Recreate the atmosphere, the discussion, the excitement, the anticipation—and yes, maybe even the nerves! This would even make a great anniversary date. Do it once a year!

24 Hotel Slumber Party

Why do we only enjoy hotels when we are traveling? Staying in a hotel is the ultimate opportunity to get away from it all without having to use your vacation days from work! If you do a search of hotels around your area, you might be surprised at the variety you'll find—different styles, different budgets, and different amenities—but they all have one thing in common: none of them have your laundry, your dishes, or your distractions! It's the perfect way to spend some one-on-one time with your sweetie.

So consider your budget, include money for snacks and beverages, and plan to pay for a movie or two. Call the hotel and ask if you need to reserve a room. Depending on where you live and what is happening in your area, some times will be easier to find a room than others.

Pack your bags and leave it all behind! (And good news—if you forget something important, you can just run home and pick it up.)

Make It Fit

- For newlyweds—If you need to spend a little less on food and entertainment, pack a picnic basket with sandwiches and snacks. You could even pack plates, dinnerware, and cups if you want it to feel more like "dinner out."
- For young parents—You don't have to stay overnight if you aren't comfortable leaving the kids or don't want to spring for an all-night babysitter. If the hotel is close to home, just spend the night at your house and come back the next day to check out. Even better—bring

the kids back the next morning and play in the pool together! Just check with the front desk ahead of time to make sure that will be okay.

- For empty nesters—If your budget allows for it, get dressed up, have room service deliver a nice, romantic dinner, and consider yourselves on a "fancy vacation" for the night.

A Couple More Ideas

- If you don't want to pay for a movie at the hotel, take your laptop with movies downloaded.
- Take a few of your favorite board games or a deck of cards.
- Are you lucky enough to have a view from your room? Take some time to sit on the balcony or by the window and daydream about a vacation you'd like to take one day! Would you like to be looking out over the ocean? The Paris skyline? Niagara Falls? Times Square? Enjoy your time to dream together!

25 Time in a Bottle

With a little planning and research, making a time capsule together will be at least two dates in one. First, when you bury your items, and second, when you dig your time capsule up in about ten years! That's called planning ahead!

The Plan

What kind of container are you going to use? It is going to be underground for a while, so consider the effects of moisture, insects, and animals. Glass won't deteriorate, but it might break. Plastic will hold up for a while, but wood will rot. Certain types of metal will rust. Some of the better options are heavy plastic with a gasket-type seal, or stainless steel with a screw top. But, as mentioned before, do your research.

Where are you going to bury your treasure? Landscapes change over time, so make sure you will be able to find your loot when you go to dig it up. If you are planning to stay in your house for a while, your backyard might be a safe bet. If you are renting or don't have a yard, would a relative's home be an option?

Suggested items to put in your time capsule (add items that mean something to you!):

- A menu from your favorite restaurant
- Movie, concert, or sporting event tickets
- A favorite CD
- A current pay stub
- A picture of your car
- A current newspaper
- Political bumper sticker or pin
- A grocery receipt
- An earring or other piece of jewelry
- An old cell phone
- A page from your planner
- A sweet note to your spouse

Items you should not include in your time capsule:

- Liquids
- Food products
- Matches
- Explosives
- Items with a strong odor (they can attract wildlife)

Above all, seal your capsule securely and place it where it cannot be ruined by water. Anything that is organic in nature (paper, wood, or fabric) should be sealed in several plastic zipper bags.

"If I could save time in a bottle, the first thing that I'd like to do Is to save every day, like a treasure and then, again, I would spend them with you."

—*Jim Croce*

26 "Board" at Home

Who says you have to leave home for laughter, fun, and competition? Board games have always provided a way to connect with each other, even while beating the pants off of your opponent. I mean, your spouse.

We are not necessarily talking about Scrabble here, although if that's your thing, go for it! Board games are not what they used to be. No longer are they about rolling the dice and racing around a colorful game board. These days they are full of strategy, alliances, and heart-stopping story lines.

So put the kids to bed early, gather some snacks, and get your game on! Below are some suggestions (search Google for the ones you aren't familiar with), but play the games that you love. As part of your date, why not run out to a department store, bookstore, or hobby store and pick out a new game to try?

- Bananagrams
- Rummikub
- Scrabble
- Jenga
- Jaipur
- Hive
- Pandemic
- Forbidden Island
- Carcassonne
- Exploding Kittens
- Would You Rather?

27 SELFIE SCAVENGER HUNT

Do you want to include another couple on a fun night out? Have a selfie scavenger hunt!

The Plan

Come up with a list of people, places, and things to take selfies with (use some of the suggestions below!) and race to the finish. Make it fair by rearranging the list so that you aren't racing to the same locations at the same time. When you have reached the last selfie on your list, text that one to your competitors (save the other selfies for later!). When that text is received, the game is over and a winner is declared! Get together (at a pre-arranged location) and share your selfies over dinner. Don't forget to take a shot of all of you together at the end of your evening!

Post your selfies on social media to give other couples a fun date night idea.

Ideas for Selfies

- A taxi driver
- A mutual friend (to both couples)
- A dog, cat, chicken, cow, or goat (depends on your location!)
- A historical marker
- A sports car (ask permission—and don't set off the car alarm!)
- An ear of corn
- A fish (live, plastic, large, small . . . It's up to you!)
- A body of water (ocean, lake, river, bathtub)

- A sports fan (wearing a team name or logo)
- A motorcycle rider (ask permission!)
- A kid doing a cartwheel (again, ask permission!)

Or make up your own! Have fun, and may the fastest selfie-taker win!

28 KIDNAPPED

Are you in need of a romantic getaway, but life keeps getting in the way? Are your phones constantly buzzing and beeping with texts, emails, and messages? Are the stresses of work, children, and family getting in the way of the most foundational relationship you have? You may have to take matters in your own hands! (Well, with a little help from your friends, that is!)

Regardless of where the stressors are coming from and who is feeling them the most, if they are affecting your time together as husband and wife, it is time to act. It's time to kidnap your sweetheart and run away for a day.

First you need a plan, accessories, a getaway car, and a safe house.

The Plan

Pre-Kidnap

- Arrange for the children (or animals) to be cared for in your absence.
- Have some cash on hand.
- Secretly inform others who need to know (boss, assistant, parent, child) and ask for their cooperation.
- Have the getaway car gassed up and ready to go. You can't run the risk of an escape at the gas station down the road.
- Arrange and prepare the safe house for your arrival. Once you get there, you won't leave again until the ransom is paid.
- What are your demands? Total disconnect from the stresses of life for twenty-four hours.

The Kidnap

- Make it quick and clean.
- Assure him or her that all will be well in twenty-four hours *if* he or she cooperates.
- Allow him or her a few minutes to tie up any loose ends. (You aren't totally uncivilized.)

- Put him or her in the getaway car, and don't stop driving until you have reached the safe house. Allow him or her snacks and a drink while in the car, but no electronics!

Once you have arrived at the safe house and closed the door behind you, there will be no more outside communication until you emerge the next day. It will be necessary for you to stay very close to your target to ensure that he or she abides by the rules and does not escape. It's a difficult assignment, but you can do it.

Enjoy!

RECREATION AND ROMANCE

In the dating world beyond dinner and a movie, you might spark something new that wasn't there before.

29 AMATEUR PHOTOGRAPHY

A walk through the neighborhood or down a local trail is often all you need to refresh your relationship. But your time together will be even more cherished (and memorable!) when you capture your adventure in photos. You do not have to be a professional or have pricey equipment in order to have a grand adventure together!

What to Bring

- Camera (even a phone camera will do!)
- A subject and a plan
- A sense of adventure
- Comfortable shoes and clothing

How to Prepare

- Be sure your camera (or phone) is fully charged and has plenty of storage space. Bring a charger that will work in your car. You will need an SD card if you want to remove some pictures in advance to create more space.
- Decide on a subject matter you both will enjoy. Are you interested in taking photos of nature? Animals? Insects? People? (Be sure to ask permission before taking pictures of people—especially children.) Maybe go for a more artsy approach and look for different color combinations, light, shapes, contrast, horizontal or vertical lines, and so on.
- Plan your location in advance. You don't want to waste your time or your creative energy driving around and looking for a place to park!

Getting Started

Loosen up! We live in a digital age, so you can take as many shots as you need to. (Some couples will remember the days when you had twenty-four attempts on a roll of film to get a good picture, but you wouldn't know if you captured any magic until your film was developed!) As a matter of fact, professionals will take hundreds of shots in order to get that one keeper. So don't be shy—snap away!

Take turns being the photographer and the assistant. Move around and experiment with different settings and light. You will be surprised at the frame-worthy photos you end up with.

Are you interested in diving in a little deeper? There are inexpensive photo editing programs for your computer and apps for your phone that can enhance, crop, colorize, brighten, or remove those unsightly blemishes, with a little practice. Some of them even have free trial periods. Of course, some of them are super complicated and will cost as much as your car—avoid those for now, unless you really catch the "bug" and decide to make this a more frequent hobby.

30 NEED FOR SPEED

Go-kart racing is a great way to infuse adrenaline and some serious fun into your dates! There are many different types of karting facilities. From the circular, low speed, family fun park to the ⅓-mile, hairpin-curve, high-speed tracks, there's a venue to fit just about any taste. Whether challenging your significant other to a fun-filled afternoon or an evening battling to earn the right to be called champion, karting is great way to build teamwork or teach your spouse some humility. Just floor the accelerator and go, go, go!

Important Tips

The best part of this activity is that you're more than likely already familiar with how to drive, so there's little to no learning curve. You may need to familiarize yourself with any safety policies and procedures ahead of time, particularly if there are any restrictions/requirements that you may need to prepare for, such as no open-toed shoes. There are usually no alcohol or controlled substance policies as well. Obviously, anyone who is pregnant, has neck or back problems, heart conditions, prone to having seizures/epilepsy, or people who should not be in stressful or physically demanding environments should consult a doctor before participating in go-kart racing.

Some karting facilities are indoors, so this fun-filled date can be enjoyed any time of the year. Depending on what part of the country you live in, the prices per race can vary from $6–$40. There may be package deals for multiple racers or races. Research the various tracks in your area to find the best fit for your comfort level, both financially and physically—then burn rubber!

31 Freshwater Fun

Renting a **sailboat** for a few hours is for the experienced sailors only. Even on a serene lake, sailing requires certain knowledge to operate the equipment on the boat and to remain safe. However, if sailing is your thing, an afternoon or evening on the open water might be just what the doctor ordered! According to Christopher Cross, "if the wind is right you can sail away and find tranquility." Renting that tranquility in a two-person sailboat (on a lake) will cost approximately $12–$15 per hour, with a possible deposit. Enjoy!

If you don't mind putting a little upper arm strength into your tranquil afternoon, check into renting a **rowboat** for you and your sweetie. It'll cost you around $8–$10 per hour, and no experience is required. The boat feels stable (not much rocking) and has room for drinks, snacks, and such. Just "row, row, row your boat gently down the stream," and it'll be a dream.

For about the same price as the rowboat, you can take a **paddleboat** out on the lake. Instead of rowing with your arms, you'll be sharing the work as both of you pedal like you are riding a bicycle. It'll cost $8–$10 per hour, and no experience is required. In the rowboat or the paddleboat, you are not very likely to get wet, but you might get very hot, so dress in casual, cool clothing.

If you are looking for a little more excitement and have experience boating in fast-moving water like a river, then a **kayak** might be your cup of tea. You can either ride together in tandem or rent single-occupancy kayaks and take the rapids on your own. These will cost $8–$10 per hour, and you are likely to get wet, so dress appropriately! If you don't have a lot of experience, you can take a kayak on the lake or pond for a more easygoing experience.

A **canoe** is the peaceful, serene sister of the kayak and will run approximately $8–$10 per hour. You can paddle together or one a time, depending on how fast you'd like to move across the water. A nighttime canoe ride might add some extra romance!

Important Note

Make sure you check (and re-check) the weather forecast before heading out to the water for any of these delightful boating dates.

32 Three-Hour Cruise

There is truly something about being on the water with your loved one that causes the cares of the world (and the cares about the kids, the job, the lawn, and the checking account) to magically float away. If you are lucky enough to have a river, stream, lake, pond, or ocean anywhere near you, grab your sweetie by the life vest and spend some time reconnecting on the water.

There are many ways to have a great date on the water! Consider these three Bs when planning your adventure:

1. Budget
2. Boating experience
3. Body of water

The Plan

A romantic dinner river cruise is perfect for a special occasion or celebration. They will usually cost around $60 per person or $150 per couple, depending on if you sit at the captain's table or at a private table for two. (You will probably also have to pay for parking at the departure point.) Dress code is "resort casual," according to most dinner cruise websites. These 2–3 hour cruises typically include the following:

- Three- or four-course dinner made to order on board
- Live music nightly
- Full bar service available
- Climate-controlled dining on multiple decks
- Open-air observation decks

33 Bird Watching

When you wake up early in the morning, they're probably the first things you hear when you head outside. During your transit to work, in the city, at the park, on your way to school, or headed back home—you can see birds just about everywhere.

Let's face it, bird watching may sound boring, but it can be so much fun once you actually experience it. There are over nine hundred species of wild birds in North America alone! The great thing about this date idea is that it can get you and your significant other back to nature to whatever degree you're comfortable with.

Getting Started

There are many ways to get started bird watching, depending on your particular skill level. If you're just looking for a fun afternoon/evening activity, all you may need is a phone with internet access and some binoculars. If you want a more complete experience, grab a bird watching guidebook.

First, select a location. This can be as simple as your backyard, a walk through your neighborhood, or a local park. It can also be a beach, lake, greenway, nature, or hiking trail, depending on what's close to you. There are many websites that can assist in locating some of the more promising spots in your area.

There are several books that you can take along to help you identify the birds you find. There are many options to choose from. Here are some of the most popular ones:

- *The Sibley Guide to Birds*, 2nd edition—one of the best sources overall

- *National Geographic Field Guide to the Birds of North America*—great field guide
- *Peterson Field Guide to Birds of North America*—traditional field guide
- *The Stokes Field Guide to the Birds of North America*—great photos
- *Kaufman Field Guide to Birds of North America*—great photos

With technology making many aspects of life more convenient, bird watching is no exception. Many of these guides have flocked to the idea of digitization so that all of the information found in that larger book can actually fit in your pocket. Here are some of the most popular digital guides:

- Audubon Birds Guide: North America
- The Sibley eGuide to Birds
- iBird
- National Geographic Birds
- Peterson Birds

Important Tips

The weather forecast is important. Dress in seasonal layers and wear comfortable walking shoes. If you find this more enjoyable than you thought you would, there are many resources available to help you have a more in-depth experience. Two are listed below. Be safe, take plenty of pictures, and enjoy the great outdoors together.

- Audubon (audubon.org)
- *BirdWatching* magazine (birdwatchingdaily.com)

34 Rock Climbing

Besides being great exercise, there are some even better reasons to try rock climbing for your next date. First of all, belaying (operating the climber's rope) requires teamwork and clear communication that can push a couple way past any mundane conversation they would have during a dinner date, and since the belayer is responsible for the climber's safety, trust is a vital part of the experience. But before you go into the mountains, try a man-made climbing wall. Your gym probably has one, or you can easily find one online.

35 ROLLER SKATING

Great music, holding hands, and a teensy bit of insecurity. All of these elements add up to a fun and romantic date. It doesn't hurt that you'll burn a few calories in the process. Maybe that will help justify the french fries and nachos from the snack bar. This is an inexpensive date—under $10 per person for admission and skate rental.

36 LASER TAG

Being in a relationship is all about teamwork, right? When playing a game of laser tag, however, you have the option of being on the same team or separate ones. Those who get a kick out of competition will enjoy the chance to earn bragging rights after the game. A laser tag date is reasonably priced at $8–$20, depending on how many rounds you play.

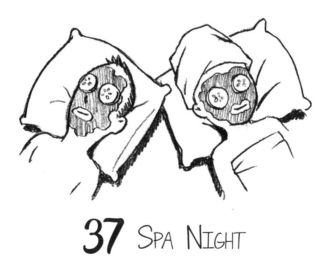

37 SPA NIGHT

Are you looking for a great way to reconnect with your spouse without the expense of a dinner out and a babysitter? How about a DIY spa night? The beauty of this idea is that you probably already have all the products you need in your kitchen and bathroom. Even if you pick up a few items from the store, the cost will be a fraction of what you'd spend on a night out, and most products, like a facial mask, will supply you with enough applications to last through more date nights!

What is the first thing you would notice if you were to walk into a high-priced day spa? The atmosphere, of course! It would feel clean, calm, comfortable, and inviting. So the first thing you'll need to do is choose a space in your home that you will turn into a spa. A bedroom with an en suite bathroom would be ideal, but your living room or dining room will work as well.

How to Prepare

- De-clutter the area completely, even if you have to put it all back after the date. There is nothing calming about looking at clutter.
- Set up candles of multiple sizes and heights around the area.
- Make a playlist of soft, relaxing music.
- Put out a couple of foot-soaking tubs (hint: use white plastic dishpans from the dollar store) and comfortable chairs.
- Matching robes are a nice touch if you have them, but if not, it's just important to be comfortable.
- Have a pair of clean, soft socks for both of you.
- Wash, dry, and fold your softest, fluffiest towels and washcloths. Have them close by.
- Mix up your DIY spa scrubs, masks, and soaking concoctions (suggestions are listed below) and put them in attractive dishes.
- Prepare some "luxurious" treats, such as chocolate-covered strawberries, truffles, nuts, and cheese.
- Have a pitcher of ice-cold lemon water in the fridge.
- Last but not least, watch a couple of videos on how to give a great foot massage and a relaxing facial massage.

The Plan

While relaxing in your robes, soak your feet in a mixture of hot water, ½ cup honey, 1 tablespoon apple cider vinegar, and a of couple lemon slices.

The honey is a humectant: it attracts and retains moisture, which is key if you want soft feet. It's also a great remedy for tired, swollen feet. Apple cider vinegar is an antibacterial remedy and a wonderful muscle relaxer. Lemons smell nice, and they are great for removing dead skin cells.

After your foot bath, try a brown sugar scrub:

Mix together 1 tablespoon each of brown sugar, baking soda, and coconut oil. Brown sugar is affordable and has an amazing, rich scent that aids in relaxation. It is also extremely moisturizing when mixed with oils and is gentle on the skin.

After scrubbing and rinsing your feet, you'll also notice that your hands are smooth and soft.

Are you ready to use those newly acquired foot massage techniques? Use more of the coconut oil for massaging and moisturizing each other's feet. Then slip on a pair of soft socks and move on to the next phase of your spa experience.

It's time to move from the feet and hands to the face. We carry tension and stress in our faces without even realizing it, until our heads are hurting and our necks are stiff. This portion of your spa night will help to ease all that tension. First, cleanse and freshen your skin. Then make a face mask.

DIY Avocado Face Mask

Ingredients

- ½ ripe avocado
- 1 Tbsp. plain yogurt
- 1 Tbsp. honey
- 2 cucumber slices

Directions

1. In shallow bowl, mash the avocado until smooth.
2. Add the yogurt and honey, and stir until combined.
3. Apply the mask evenly to each other's faces, then sit back and allow the mask to set for about 15 minutes. Rinse with warm water and pat dry.

Now that you each have clean skin, make sure your hands are washed before touching your partner's face. Use a video for guidance on how to massage the face, temples, and scalp for tension relief. Take turns trying out these techniques on your spouse.

By the end of this date, you and your sweetheart are going to be relaxed and free from the cares of the world! At least for the evening. Be sure to blow out all the candles before you get so relaxed that you fall asleep!

38 THE AMAZING RACE
(Double Date)

Your local supercenter will be the backdrop for a double date that you won't forget. It's a race to the finish, and the winner buys dinner!

How It Works

Each couple will take their own shopping cart and head off together to locate ten items from various departments within the store. The more obscure the item, the better. Once ten items have been located, the team will go to the front of the store (or another designated meeting place) and wait for their opponents to arrive.

Once both teams are finished with their search, it is time to swap carts! It's now a race to put all the items back in their proper location on the shelf and be the first team to get back to the cart return with an empty cart!

Play by the rules! You are going to be on the honor system when you are putting them items away, so no cheating! If you have to return a bottle of shampoo, you can't just leave it randomly in the health and beauty section. You must place it back on the shelf where it came from, with the matching brand and size. And no asking for help from the store associates! You and your spouse are on your own to locate homes for all of your items.

Now are you ready for an entertaining evening that will not only build teamwork but build friendships as well? On your mark, get set, GO!

39 Tour de Neighborhood

You've heard of the "Tour de France" right? Well, our version is not a competition, and it's not in France, but it's definitely a winner! A bike ride is a fantastic way to spend a little time together.

How to Prepare

- This may seem obvious, but check your tires and make sure both bikes are in good working condition. Its not as much fun to push a bike as it is to ride one.
- Make sure you both have a helmet that fits properly and is comfortable. Some states even have laws regarding wearing head protection while riding in certain areas, so just wear the helmet.
- Throw a couple of water bottles in a lightweight backpack, especially if you are riding in a hot climate. Nothing kills the romance like a heat stroke.
- Plan a stopping point—a local cafe, park, bakery (just incase you burn too many calories!)—and make sure you have a place to park and lock up your bikes.

There is no need to rush this date, unless you are just feeling the need for speed. Especially if you are riding in your own neighborhood or close to home, take the time to notice interesting trees, buildings, and how nice your neighbor's lawn looks. During our daily commute, we tend to speed past the things in our neighborhoods that make them unique and special. This is a great opportunity to discover new reasons together to love your home and your time together.

40 TIPTOE THROUGH THE TULIPS

This date feels relaxing, looks heavenly, and even smells glorious! Almost all of your senses will wake up on a walk through a botanical garden together. And the selfies will even be beautiful!

Now, before you roll your eyes and think to yourself, "This is going to be the most boring date of my life!" just keep in mind the following: a study on the science of attraction found that women are more likely to find a man attractive if they're surrounded by beautiful flowers.[1] Walking hand in hand down paths of mood-lifting blooms could surely be the romantic highlight of your week!

Important Tips

Depending on your location, ticket prices range from free to moderate (up to $25), and there are often discounts available for couples, on weekdays, or during the winter.

Dress comfortably (wear good shoes!) but not too casual, keeping in mind that this would be a lovely place to take some pictures of each other and your surroundings. If you're permitted to bring drinks and food into the gardens, pack some water or other beverages and a small snack for you and your partner. If there are picnic areas or open grass areas, take a blanket along.

If you'd like to add an extra element of romance to the date, bring along a book of poetry, and after you find a nice, secluded place to relax for a few minutes, take turns reading to each other.

1. Nicolas Guéguen, "'Say it . . . Near the Flower Shop': Further Evidence of the Effect of Flowers on Mating," *The Journal of Social Psychology* 152, no. 5 (2012): 529–532.

41 WALK BESIDE ME AND BE MY FRIEND

Sometimes the best date is a relaxing walk together, holding hands side by side. Why? First of all, it's better exercise than watching another movie on the couch. Secondly, you can talk about nothing in particular, talk about something important, or not talk at all, but at least you are connected and together. And last but not least, when you slow down enough to stroll down a street or path, there are always things to discover. And noticing something for the first time together is an automatic cherished memory—even it it's nothing more than an interesting insect or a tree you never saw before.

Do scope out your walking route ahead of time so you know you'll be safe and you'll find your way back. It can be a country path or a city sidewalk.

Do wear comfy shoes and clothing, and be aware of hills or obstacles along the way.

Don't walk with your phone in your hand. No matter what, you will check it at least once. And this is "us" time. Leave "them" out of it. (Keep your phone in your pocket, though, in case of emergencies.)

Don't wear earbuds and listen to music. While a nice soundtrack in the background can add to the mood, it also distracts you from each other and might block out noise that you need to hear (e.g., cars, busses, trains, lions, tigers, or bears).

Don't cancel your walk if it rains! Just grab and umbrella and enjoy the sounds and smells of a shower.

> *"Don't walk behind me; I may not lead. Don't walk in front of me;*
> *I may not follow. Just walk beside me and be my friend."*
>
> —*Albert Camus*

42 Zootopia

A trip to a large zoo is exciting and memorable, but often it is expensive and exhausting as well. So if you are married to an animal lover, and you are living on a budget, another option might be your local petting zoo!

Important Tips

- Do a bit of research on the petting zoos in your area, and check out their online reviews and operating hours.
- Check the weather forecast. Rain can easily make any fun day at the zoo turn into a sloppy, muddy disaster, so try to schedule the date for a dry day with some sunshine. Because you'll be outside most of the time, it would be best to avoid the hottest days of summer and the coldest days of winter.
- Wear comfortable shoes that you don't mind getting dirty, and dress in clothes that can survive a cow snuggle and a curious goat.
- Be aware of your surroundings, follow staff instructions, and be brave! A petting zoo is all about getting up close and personal with the animals, so jump in and be sure to get some pictures. If this date is lots of fun for you, bring the kids back next time you come!

43 Horsing Around

What is it about horseback riding that is so romantic? Maybe it's the quiet tranquility of the setting, or maybe Hollywood had something to do with it. It's probably not the smells. But regardless, a trail ride on the beach or through a forest or countryside is a date to remember.

Important Tips

If you and your sweetie are not experienced riders, you'll want to look for a reputable riding company or stable with experienced guides. Some stables will offer group rides, but depending on your budget, you may want a private instructor for a little more "alone time" and a little more romance. A 30 minute group-ride with a guide will start at around $30, and go up from there. So even though this date may not be the least expensive, the romance-factor makes it worth every penny.

The weather forecast is important. A trail ride in the rain or a storm that spooks the horses will put an end to your fun, pronto! Dress in comfortable layers and wear boots if you have them. If your ride extends into the evening hours, it could get chilly. Wear a hat (a cowboy hat if you can find one!) and bring sunglasses. Bring water bottles and your cell phone (charged up!) in case of emergencies.

If your ride is a longer one, check with the riding company to see if a picnic lunch would be appropriate. It would give you two a chance to chat and the horses an opportunity to rest up before they have to hit the dusty trail to bring you back to reality.

Be safe. Take pictures. Enjoy the scenery. And giddy-up!

44 Up, Up, and Away!

While a hot air balloon ride may not be something you and your sweetheart can do every week, it is certainly something you should consider for a special occasion. This one-in-a-lifetime experience is truly the date to end all dates, and it's absolutely worth saving for.

There are probably more balloon companies than you realize, so if you are considering this idea to romance your sweetie, take some time to shop around and do your homework to find a reputable company with a certified pilot. It will cost quite a bundle—usually between $150 and $300 per person, depending on where you are in the country. The high-dollar markets will obviously be more expensive, so if you live in a large metropolitan area, consider taking a ride out to a neighboring community where prices might be a little less, or you can look online for coupons.

Important Tips

Hot air balloon rides usually take place at sunrise or just before sunset, when the weather is coolest and the winds are the calmest, and you should allow about three hours from start to finish. This includes getting the balloon ready for launch, the approximately one-hour-long balloon flight, and packing everything up at your destination.

Wear casual clothing that's suited to the temperature, along with comfortable outdoor shoes. You'll likely be walking through a field to climb into the basket, so don't wear sandals, heels, flip-flops, or open-toed shoes. Wear light layers so that you can easily adjust to the temperature changes.

Depending on how romantic you want this adventure to be, you can charter a private flight with you and your sweetheart, or, if you'd like to save a little money and you are up for making new friends, you can book a couple of spaces with another group. Either way, the experience will be breathtaking, so if you can't quite swing the private flight, don't worry.

You will want to take pictures! Remember to bring your camera to get some good footage of your trip and to preserve those memories for a lifetime. You might want to consider a camera strap of some kind, though, so you don't drop your camera over the side!

What to Expect

When the burner is off, it is extremely quiet. Peace and quiet is one of the most enjoyable aspects of ballooning. You'll likely even be able to hear ground noises. Are you afraid of heights? Get motion sickness easily? You should definitely bring those things to the attention of the pilot, but don't let them keep you from giving it a shot. Most people report that those sensations don't bother them at all in a hot air balloon. As a matter of fact, since you are moving with the breeze, it doesn't even feel windy at all.

Because of the expense, this adventure is obviously not for everyone. But if you have the ability to put this special date together, you will have a cherished memory to last a lifetime.

45 Take the Scenic Route

During autumn, when the air becomes crisp and the leaves become fiery shades of gold, orange, and red, a simple drive along the countryside or on a mountain road could be a delightful way to spend some time with your sweetheart.

The Plan

Take a long, relaxed drive through the most picturesque areas near you. If you aren't sure where to go, check with your local forestry service or just ask around, but choose a lovely route. Autumn is an absolutely gorgeous time of year, and an afternoon spent enjoying the scenery is one of the most romantic and relaxed you could hope for!

- Play some good music. You don't want it to be too relaxing since you're going to be driving, but choose some tunes that make you feel lighthearted and happy, maybe even something nostalgic.
- Pack some snacks and maybe a cooler with soft drinks or water. Finger foods will be easy to munch on while you're driving. Bring along a blanket in case you come across a good picnic spot.
- Choose roads that allow you to pull over frequently and that are known for having few cars. Appreciate the view! The emptier the path, the slower you'll be able to drive and the more you'll both get out of the experience! Take a camera along to capture the beauty around you.

Important Tips

- This trip will be much more enjoyable in a nice, clean car. Clean it out and make sure it smells nice before you begin your journey. Maybe you could even take it for a professional detailing.
- If your trip will take you through rural areas, be sure and have an actual paper map! GPS maps are wonderful until you drive through an area with no service and realize that you have no idea where you are or how to get where you are going! Plan ahead and have a backup.

Remember, this is one outing for which arriving at a destination is unimportant—it's all about the path you take.

46 TAKE ME HOME, COUNTRY ROADS

Have you ever wondered what your spouse was like as a child? Can you picture them riding a bike or climbing a tree? This date will give you a chance to learn more about each other by sharing childhood memories. Spend some time together driving down memory lane and you'll see each other in a whole new light!

The Plan

If you live close enough to the town or city where you or your spouse grew up, pack a lunch, hop in the car, and buckle up! With a little pre-planning, you'll get to see a side of your spouse that you've never seen before!

Where to Go

- The house where you grew up
- Your elementary or middle school
- A park you played at
- The tree you loved to climb
- The house of your childhood best friend

How to Prepare

- Roads and landmarks change over time, so don't depend on your memory to get you where you want to go! Gather addresses of those memorable locations ahead of time and plug them into your GPS.
- Create a playlist of great songs that bring back favorite memories to share. Your first slow dance? Your cheerleading routine? Your first kiss?
- Plan some conversation starters to make your driving time more interesting. Who was your favorite teacher and why? What was your curfew, and what happened when you missed it? What is your earliest memory? Who was your best friend?

Crank up your playlist of music that will remind you of those carefree times "back in the day." Sing along and enjoy the journey! Pull out your conversation starters, and let the memories flow. Take in as many "historical" sites as you can on your journey back in time together. Take pictures, ask questions, and really listen. Encourage your spouse to "ramble," and don't rush them. Let them talk as much as their memories and your time will allow—and soak it all in. Talk to some locals. Try to imagine your husband or wife as a little boy or little girl. This is a glimpse of your spouse that you may have never seen before!

Make It Fit

- For newlyweds—Have a pre-date chat with your mother-in-law to find out the name of a favorite childhood pal, and set up a surprise reunion over lunch or dinner. Be sure to take a picture and exchange contact information so you can stay in touch!

- For young parents—If you can't get away long enough to take a road trip, locate your old yearbooks. Flip through the pages and reminisce about old friends and youthful adventures. Since you can't be there in person, be sure to share stories with lots of details. Pick out a couple of old friends you'd like to catch up with, and take turns looking them up on social media.

- For empty nesters—If time and budget allow for an overnight stay, take some extra time to look around your hometown. Make a detailed record of your trip, the locations you visit, and the memories you share—either with a video or in a journal. Share your travelogue and your stories with your children or your grandchildren when you see them next.

47 Take a Hike

Whether you're on your first date or celebrating your fortieth anniversary, going on a hike together offers endless opportunities for romance and relaxation. A planned hike is a great way to say "I love you." By leaving your everyday lives at home and having an adventure together, it can bring a new vigor and excitement to your relationship.

What's so fun about getting sweaty and tired? A romantic hike is not only about reaching a destination—although working together to accomplish a challenging goal certainly will get the adrenaline going—it's also about the little thoughtful details and tender mercies along the way. Watching a sunset side by side, stumbling across a beautiful stream or pond, or discovering what you are sure is a new species of insect all make good memories and great photos.

What to Bring

- Rolled blanket (or even a yoga mat!) so that you have a warm, dry place to sit next to each other
- Thermos of hot chocolate if you are hiking in the cooler weather months
- Water bottle filled with homemade flavored water
- Treat that your sweetie wouldn't expect, like fruit, fancy cheeses, hummus, and pita
- First-aid supplies for unexpected bites, cuts, scrapes, blisters, or sprains (If you know your spouse has allergies, come prepared for that as well. Nothing will spoil your romantic plans like a trip to the emergency room!)
- Clean towels and wipes

The Plan

Choose a destination that can easily be reached by car or by foot. Seclusion is nice, but getting lost is not! Check your state's forestry department website or your local parks and recreation department if you aren't sure where to start looking.

Set a pace that is comfortable for both of you, and suggest frequent rest breaks to enjoy the scenery. This is not a triathlon; there are no prizes for finishing first, and there is no schedule.

Enjoy the quiet time with your date—no children, no responsibilities, no stress. Don't worry if you aren't chattering constantly. Just be together.

Add Some Romance

- Go out the day before your hike and plant a treasure for your sweetie to find. A small gift or something sentimental to you both will show your spouse how much your time together means to them.
- Surprise your partner by hiking to a pre-planned destination for an overnight stay. Can you imagine your spouse's elation when you

stumble upon a cabin that you have reserved and already stocked with flowers, treats, and bedding, or a campground with tents and a fire pit that were set up in advance?

With a bit of planning and preparation, this date will be a memory to share—and perhaps recreate—often!

48 ON A WING AND A PRAYER

Butterflies are not only beautiful, but they are also symbolic of transition, resurrection, hope, and life. They take our minds and hearts to a place of joy and freedom, often reminding us of a more carefree time in our lives when anything seemed possible. Wouldn't it be a lovely refresher for your relationship to spend an afternoon date at a butterfly farm?

If you have never experienced the beauty of a butterfly farm, you are truly missing out on one of the more beautiful miracles that nature has to offer. There are fully functioning farms in almost every state, and if yours doesn't have one, you can most certainly find an exhibit or a butterfly garden at a museum or zoo. It is worth the search!

What to Expect

- **Cost:** Usually under $10 per person
- **How it works:** Call ahead to ask about group tours and self-guided tours. Reservations may or may not be needed, and be sure to check their calendar for special events.
- **Time needed:** Plan to spend about 2–3 hours there, depending on the size of your exhibit and your group. Arrive early to allow for parking and check-in.

- **Weather:** Some butterfly farms are completely outdoors, while some smaller exhibits are in a more sheltered environment. If your tour is totally outside, weather could cause a cancellation or a very unpleasant visit, so call ahead to check on policies regarding weather.

Important Tips

- Schools will often take field trips to butterfly farms, so if you want a more romantic experience with your date, you may want to ask ahead to find out your best opportunity for some quiet time.
- Don't bring your pets. Dogs and hundreds of butterflies do not work well together.
- Bring your camera! You won't find a better location for photos, and you'll want to capture this time you spend together.
- If you or your spouse suffers from plant-based or pollen-based allergies, this may not be the date for you. Check with the farm, but keep in mind that a butterfly's main responsibility in its short life is to cross-pollinate!

A date to a butterfly farm or garden could provide the transformation or even the resurrection that your marriage needs!

49 LET'S GET PHYSICAL

If you do not already belong to a gym, use this date to get physical (and healthy) together!

Many gyms offer a free trial, so do a little research ahead of time. Choose a location based on your fitness level and your comfort. If you have never set foot near a free-weight and wouldn't know a protein shake from a McDonald's milkshake, don't choose the gym where the bodybuilders hang out. It might be a good idea to call ahead, describe yourself and your spouse, and ask the gyms if they have a program for you. Tell them this is a one-time trial and you are looking for a gym to start using.

And remember—this is not a time to hurt yourself or prove anything! This is a time to encourage each other and work together. Getting healthy together is a great way to say, "I love you, and I want you to be beside me for a long, long time!"

Hit a smoothie bar before your workout for some energizing fuel, but be sure to stay away from heavy, fatty foods. Then take a deep breath, hold hands, and go get sweaty together!

50 COME FLY WITH ME

It doesn't take much effort or money to arrange an afternoon of entertainment. There are times when dressing up to attend an entertaining play followed by a wonderful dinner in an expensive restaurant just isn't as much fun as spending a couple of dollars on a date that takes you and your spouse to an open field for an afternoon. Oh how much fun it was to fly a kite when you were young! Create some new memories with your spouse with this simple but magical endeavor.

First, decide whether you and your spouse feel more comfortable making your own kite or purchasing one. Making your own offers more creative control over your kite, and you can find plenty of ideas and instructions online. If you and your spouse find creating something together synergistic, get creative! Make a six-foot tall box kite, a flying octopus, or whatever you feel inspired to make. Purchasing a kite, will give you more time together actually flying it. Whether you build a kite together or pick one up at a local hobby shop, working together to get your kite in the air and then watching it soar will make for a fun and meaningful date!

51 Just Dance

Push the sofa back, turn on the home game system, and get ready to dance like nobody's watching! Take turns picking the songs, and try to keep up with the game. Music, moves, and just a teensy bit of competition make for a fun living room date!

The Rules of the Evening

1. No laughing at your spouse, but laughing *with* them is perfectly acceptable! As a matter of fact, it's expected!
2. Put the kids to bed! You wouldn't take them to a dance club with you, right? Well, your living room is about to turn into Studio 54, so only the grown-ups are allowed—unless you need them to show you how to turn the game on, of course.
3. So nobody is going to confuse you with Michael Jackson? Or Fred Astaire, if that's your generation? Don't worry! The key is to match the moves you see on the screen. No creativity needed! As long as the game "sees" you moving in the same general way, you score points. How much you "get into it" is totally up to you!
4. You have to put your heart into it! You are in your home, and nobody is watching. (Except possibly your sweetie, who is making a video to share on social media.) So crank up the volume, stand up, and *get down*!

It might be a good idea to eat a late dinner *after* you've danced the night away. You're going to want a rest and a cool down after you leave the dance floor. If you aren't used to moving like that, be prepared to help each other out of bed the next morning! Laughing is permitted then too!

52 It's a Marvelous Night for a Moon Dance

Sometimes the best places to take your date are right under you nose! In this case, with a little ingenuity and creativity, your backyard will become the hottest nightspot in town. This date is a little bit sneaky and a lot romantic, but just keep humming a Van Morrison tune in your head while you prepare, and you'll get the idea.

How to Prepare

String some Christmas lights in the backyard, and make a romantic playlist on your device. Set up a small table (with a table cloth) and two chairs. Put a single flower in a vase, and set the table with pretty stemware filled with your favorite beverage, a couple of cloth napkins, and a plate of romantic *hors d'oeuvres* (e.g., chocolate-covered strawberries).

Tell your date to dress up for a romantic evening, and pick him or her up at the front door. Put a blindfold on your spouse, and with your surprise safely hidden, walk your date around to the backyard, where you have staged a beautiful and romantic evening. With the music playing, remove the blindfold and ask for a dance. You can figure out the rest from here.

Variations

Don't have a backyard? What about a rooftop? The beach? A friend's yard? The important parts of this date are the preparation, the element of surprise, and of course, the moonlight. So be sneaky and be romantic. Neither of you will soon forget this night!

53 Horse-Drawn Carriage Ride

On a warm summer evening or a snowy winter night, nothing says romance like a horse-drawn carriage ride through town. You might even learn some things that you didn't know about the town, the horse, and each other!

Prices can vary greatly based on the season and the city. Depending on the company, they will charge either per person or per ride, so you'll want to be clear about what you are getting ahead of time. Find a reputable company online or through word of mouth.

54 Spooky Stroll

Almost every city has some kind of haunted history, and most have guided tours of these of spooky spots. You don't have to wait until Halloween to have goose bumps on your interlocked arms! Search your local historic sites or downtown organization to find the tour that's right for you.

Important Tips

- Usually the tours are about 1–2 hours in length, and you will be walking/standing the entire time. Dress accordingly, with comfortable shoes. Haunted tours are usually held "rain or shine," so plan ahead for the weather, and check the company's policy on refunds.
- If you are more interested in the historical significance of the locations you will visit on your tour, go during the day! Most of the tour companies offer at least one or two afternoon tours on the weekends.
- If you consider getting the *daylights scared out of you* to be a good time, then find an evening tour. The eerie glow of candlelight, a light breeze, and the stories of local history and lingering spirits will be sure to have your hair standing on end!

55 STARRY, STARRY NIGHT

Stargazing has been associated with romance and love since long before Van Gogh painted his famous image of the night sky. If you want to sweep that special someone off their feet, you can't do better than planning an evening of gazing at some of the most wondrous creations!

Weather conditions, location, and timing should all be considered when planning an evening of stargazing. Crystal clear skies are a necessity for seeing the universe's most spectacular light show.

- **Weather:** In order to see as many stars as possible, check the weather report ahead of time for high nighttime visibility. Many international websites offer satellite and radar forecasts tailored to astronomers.
- **Location:** Dark skies are best, so leave cities and large towns behind and travel to more rural or remote areas far from artificial light and excess pollution.
- **Timing:** While full moons can be romantic in and of themselves, they light up the sky in such a way that makes stars harder to see. Opt for a time of the month when the moon is small. In most climates, winter often presents the clearest night skies.

How to Prepare

Bring a blanket to lie on while you stare up at the sky, snacks and drinks, soft background music, and binoculars (these are optional—you probably won't need them).

Learn about how to find stars, planets, and constellations. Bring along a book or astrological map to help with your search.

Whether you spot anything you can identify or you wish upon a shooting star, the most important thing is that you spend time admiring the majesty of the night sky and the beauty of your marriage!

56 SHOOTING RANGE

Who says that a date always has to be about cuddling, snuggling, or eating? This outing may be just the thing to knock the dust off of date night. Go online to find a shooting range near you. Just be sure to do some research to make sure you find a range that fits your needs. The staff can help you feel more confident about handling the firearms and understanding safety procedures.

The good indoor ranges are designed for safety and comfort with climate-controlled shooting lanes. They usually rent out some of the most popular firearms and ammunition. If you need to rent a handgun, free test fires on handguns and long guns may be available so you can see which model feels best to you.

There are often specials for certain days of the week or times of the day as well. And if you find yourself enjoying it, certified instructors that offer classes for all experience levels may be available.

You may just want to try it for the experience of saying that you did it, or if you're more experienced, you may want to add an element of competition to your evening by seeing who can get the tightest grouping of shots in a certain area of the target. There are a variety of reasons people enjoy visiting shooting ranges, including (but not limited to) education, protection, recreation, competition, or stress relief. It's also a great way to bond with your spouse over some hot lead and shredded targets.

57 CAMPING

How much more romantic can it get than sitting next to a fire and looking up at a starry sky? If you've tried and failed in the past to add a spark of romance to your dates again, try the ideas listed below to add some much needed fuel to the romance in your marriage.

- **Double Sleeping Bag:** Yes, that's right—a sleeping bag built for two. Or you could just zip two regular sleeping bags together. Either way, it will be much more fun cuddling up together than sleeping in individual bags. Be sure to bring a blanket as well. It will help warm things up even more when you're sitting next to the fire.
- **Portable/Bluetooth Speaker:** Nothing will add to the mood already set by the stars, fresh air, and campfire more than the perfect playlist. Create your playlist ahead of time using you and your spouse's favorite romantic tunes. Having speakers that make it actually sound good instead of like an old AM radio being played out of a single speaker in the dashboard of an Oldsmobile will make all the difference.
- **Location:** Be sure to plan ahead and find a spot that isn't heavily populated. Nothing can ruin an romantic get away like a family with four kids running through your campsite every fifteen minutes. The setting should be romantic as well: a lake or river, mountains or hills, wooded but able to see enough sky so that the sunset and sunrise are visible.
- **Disconnect/Reconnect:** It's vital to disconnect from your everyday life and experience this moment with your spouse. Until you put away your phone, your spouse will feel as though they have to share you with whoever may try to contact you, even if you disregard the notifications. Nothing says "I love you" like your undivided attention. There is nothing more important to improving your marriage than giving your time and attention. Make this trip about nothing but strengthening your marriage.

- **Food:** Because you're in the woods, you may need to plan ahead in order to have a romantic dinner, but it doesn't need to be complicated. Is there a meal that has special meaning to the both of you? Something you had on your honeymoon or your first date? I remember we had cheese hotdogs on our first date. They were disgusting, but they hold a special place in both our hearts now. Be sure to pack their favorite dessert as well.
- **Activities:** Pack various games (card games, board games, dice games, etc.), reading materials, a guitar or ukulele if one of you plays, art materials for capturing that perfect sunrise, and a notebook and pen to write down any special moments you don't want to forget.

You'll find that leaving much of the plans a mystery to your spouse will intensify the romance and make the adventure that much more memorable.

Check with the National Recreation Reservation Service for a list of campgrounds in your state, as well as the amenities available there. There are campgrounds with amenities like restrooms, showers, and even electricity for any additional strings of lights you'd like to hang to add to the mood. Your spouse will really appreciate all the thought, time, and effort you put into this romantic getaway.

58 Dine-In at a Drive-In

Finding a drive-in movie theater may not be as commonplace as it used to be, but with a little research and preparation, this date will be worth the extra effort.

Google it! There are still a few operating drive-in theaters around the country. So if you are lucky enough to have one near you, it's easy enough to find online.

How to Prepare

- Check the movie times.
- Check the weather beforehand. Most of the time, a theater won't be open if it's supposed to rain that evening.
- Keep seasonal issues in mind. It may take some extra planning to accommodate hot weather, cold weather, and so on.
- Pack some blankets or chairs if you're planning to sit outside of the vehicle.
- Pack some favorite foods for a picnic or an after-dinner snack. Many theaters show double features, so be sure to take enough food/refreshments and plan accordingly for that amount of time.

59 Dancing in the Streets

Whether you live in a small town or a large city, every season of the year has festivals and street fairs associated with it, and that is something worth celebrating in the streets about! If you and your spouse have a free afternoon and some good walking shoes, check out one of your local street festivals on your next date.

During the warmer months of the year, you'll be hard-pressed to find a weekend when there isn't a street festival happening somewhere. Festivals will celebrate arts, cultures, history, food, music, and dancing. Some will feature all of them! No matter what you're looking for, you can probably find a festival that suits your fancy by throwing a dart at a map, but thankfully that isn't necessary. An internet search will work just fine.

How to Prepare

- Street fairs usually span many blocks, so come prepared to do a lot of walking.
- Bring a backpack with a water bottle and cleansing wipes (or hand sanitizer) in case you need to freshen up or clean your hands before a quick snack.
- Wear a hat and sunscreen.
- Be sure to bring along cash, since most vendors don't take cards or checks. Be prepared to pay cash for parking as well.
- If your festival includes performances or shows of any kind, there should be a schedule online or at the gate so that you can plan your day around which ones you want to see.
- Allow several hours to take it all in, but keep in mind that restroom facilities are usually the portable kind, and there is usually a line!
- If you have any gift-giving occasions coming up, a street fair is a fantastic place to find unique, one-of-a-kind gifts! If you take some time to ask questions and talk with the vendors, you'll likely find some pretty fascinating backstories as well.

With all of your preparation, you are ready to enjoy all your street festival has to offer, taking in the sights, sounds, and smells hand-in-hand, making life-long memories!

60 Garden Party

Are you willing to get your hands dirty and put in a little sweat equity to make something lovely together? Isn't that what marriage is all about anyway? This date will cost you a small amount of time, energy, and money, but in the end, the payoff will be bright and sunny!

In the early spring months, after the last frost of the season, is the best time to make a trip to the garden center. By this time, most of us are over and done with the cold winter temperatures and are ready to get our hands into the warm spring soil! Spend some time choosing a special spot in the yard, gather all the necessary tools, and then spend a couple of hours together soaking in the sun and planting a beautiful flower garden. After you are done, you will have created a beautiful reminder that the two of you can accomplish wonders together!

When the work is done and the tools are put away, grab a couple of ice-cold beverages, put a couple of chairs or benches out by your new garden, and enjoy your handiwork!

61 I Don't Want to Grow Up!

Are the two of you just sick to death of "adulting," and you need to turn back the clock to a much simpler time and relive your favorite childhood experiences? Well, this date is for you!

If you have children, you probably have the best park in town under your "frequent locations" on your GPS. You know the one—it has the tallest slide, the best merry-go-round, and the smoothest swings. If you're lucky, it also has some awesome monkey bars and a seesaw.

Pack your backpack (yes, your backpack!) with a couple of ziplock bags full of crackers and fruit snacks. If you are going at mealtime, then pack a couple of PB&J sandwiches. And don't forget the juice boxes! A kid can get very thirsty on the playground!

Once you get there, you have permission to act like a child. Swing, slide, run, jump, scream, and squeal! Spin on the merry-go-round until you get nauseous, and ride on the seesaw until you're sore! Then take a break and find a picnic table to enjoy your treats. Sometimes a few childish moments are all the doctor ordered to get us back into a grown-up state of mind. No arguing over the front seat when you get back into the car!

62 Private (Backyard) Resort

How can you have a quiet afternoon or evening together by the pool if you don't have a pool? With a little imagination and a small investment, you can be lounging by the soothing waters at your own (homemade) resort by dinnertime!

Large department stores and toy stores have wading pools for approximately $15–$40, depending on size, shape, and material. And after your pool-side date is over, the kids or the family dog can get plenty of use out of it during the hot summer months. What a great investment!

This date only requires a few more items to make it a success. If you were going to spend an afternoon at the community pool, what would you take?

- Towels
- Pool Chairs
- Sunscreen
- Sunglasses
- Music
- A cooler with drinks and snacks

Try to forget that you are going to be in your backyard, and don't allow any of your typical home responsibilities to distract you (no weeding the garden or taking a quick break to fold the laundry!). Enjoy your time together as you escape to your private poolside resort. Every good marriage requires a bit of imagination, right?

63 Baby, You Can Drive My Car

It's time to live the dream! Have you always wanted to drive a certain sports car or luxury car? Well, the cost of renting a car for the day is approximately what it would cost you for a nice dinner and a movie . . . but it's a lot more fun!

This date is especially good for the newlywed couple on a budget who are used to driving on bald tires with no air conditioning or the couple who drives a minivan with multiple car seats, Cheerios in the carpet, and an old CD player rocking Disney soundtracks.

The Plan

- Use Google or use the phone to check around your area. Different rental-car agencies will have different cars, rates, and rules, so spend a day or two researching.
- Once you've found your dream car, make a reservation for the day you plan to have your date. Make sure that both of you are on the contract so you can both have a chance to drive.
- Pick up the car as early as you can that day so you can enjoy it for the full rental period. You also need time to familiarize yourself with all the gadgets and technology that the car has to offer.

- Decide where you want to go. Are you looking forward to the open road? Or do you want to cruise the city streets and show off your ride? Either way, make sure you won't be charged for extra mileage according to the contract.

Ready, set, go! Spend the day living like a celebrity, and enjoy the looks and waves you get from admirers on the road. Talk about your dream cars, crank up the tunes, and set the cruise control. Just make sure you get it back before it turns into a pumpkin (and your credit card takes another hit)!

Wouldn't it be a blast to take your luxury car to the drive-in for a movie before you have to turn it in? That would be more comfortable than movie theater seats! Have fun!

SENTIMENT AND SERVICE

In sharing love with others, we grow our capacity to feel love for each other.

64 DOING GOOD, FEELING GOOD

The couple that volunteers together stays together! No matter how long you've been married, volunteering can help you maintain a meaningful and caring relationship. Spending time in the service of others is a powerful bonding experience, and scheduling time to volunteer together will strengthen your companionship and give you plenty to talk about. It also helps you count your blessings. Working together for others who are in need can help you and your partner see all the good in the lives you share together and gain perspective about your problems.

Finding the right volunteer opportunities. Once you begin your search for volunteer opportunities in your area, you may quickly become overwhelmed with the sheer volume of the needs in your community. A random internet search will possibly take you in too many directions and might lead you to unscrupulous organizations who want to take advantage of your kindness. For this purposes, you may want to start with the following reputable and well-known organizations:

- The United Way (unitedway.org)
- Just Serve (justserve.org)
- The Red Cross (redcross.org)
- Habitat for Humanity (habitat.org)

65 Deliver a Date

Have you ever heard the saying, "The best way to find love is to give it away"? This date night idea will do just that. Not only will you give your "date" away to a deserving couple so they can find or rekindle their love, but you will find greater love for each other in the process! Do you know of another couple that could use a date night, but for some reason or another, they just can't seem to make it happen? Maybe they just had a baby, maybe they have a house full of children and never find the time to get out, or maybe they are newlyweds who are living on ramen noodles and hot dogs. Perhaps they are elderly and just don't have the energy to get out the door anymore. It's time to make that much-needed date happen! Special note: Parts of this idea will depend on how well you know the family you choose to surprise and how familiar you are with their schedule, their habits, and their children. This may feel a bit awkward if they are not close friends.

Step One: Setting the Stage

If you can pull this one off as a surprise, it's even more fun, but once you choose your "victim," you definitely want to call ahead to make sure they are home and dressed for company! You could try saying something like, "What time do you usually eat dinner? I have something I'd like to drop off, and I don't want to interrupt." Once you get that answer, you're armed with all you need for the next step!

Step Two: The Meal

This part has some flexibility. If there is a special dish that you know this couple would love and you have the time and resources to bake it, by all means, do it! If you are able to pick up a nice meal from a restaurant that they like, then do that. If they like pizza, that would work as well. Honestly, the meal is not as important as the atmosphere you are going to create in the next step. But don't forget desert! (Be sure to be mindful of any food allergies and foods that they dislike.)

Step Three: The Atmosphere

This is the fun part. Pack up a nice tablecloth, a couple of your best dinner settings, silverware, glassware, a bud vase (don't forget the flower), a candle, and a lighter or match. You'll want some romantic music as well. Also include in your basket something for after dinner, like a movie to watch or a game they can play.

Step Four: The Delivery

Show up at the house about an hour before they usually eat dinner, holding your baskets (food and supplies). When they come to the door, tell them that their date night has arrived! If they'll let you in the door at this point, go ahead and set the table, put out the food, light the candles, and turn on the music. Tell them they should spend a little time together and that you've taken care of everything!

Step Five: The Exit

If they have children, be prepared to take the kids with you to a local park or to your place to watch movies and have popcorn. Let their parents know what time you'll be bringing them back. If there are no children in the home, then wish your friends well and make your exit quickly.

Most of all, be relaxed and flexible and have fun with this. The more comfortable you are with this idea, the more your friends will be able to enjoy this unexpected blessing. Spread the love!

66 Deliver Meals to the Elderly

Many local food banks and charities provide this service for the elderly. Hot meals are packaged and ready to serve. You are given a route that will take you a couple of hours to complete. Many of the elderly that you will deliver this hot meal to are shut-ins and may have no other face-to-face interaction during their week. Most organizations, however, do discourage entering the home of the person for liability reasons, but you will make their day with a smile and a delicious meal.

67 Big Brothers Big Sisters

Give the gift of friendship to a child! Being a Big Brother or Big Sister is one of the most enjoyable and fulfilling things you'll ever do. You can help shape a child's future for the better by empowering him or her to achieve. And the best part is that it's actually a lot of fun. You and your new friend can share the kinds of activities you already like to do. Together you can be powerful role models to a child and rediscover your silly side.

68 Volunteer at a Homeless Shelter

Volunteering at a homeless shelter is very rewarding, and there is a wide variety of ways you can help out, such as by serving food, picking up donations, teaching skills, talking to people, and more. Nothing will put your life back into perspective like spending time serving the homeless. And it's a great opportunity to spread some joy to those who might not have much to be thankful for.

69 Volunteer at a Senior Center

As a couple, you can visit seniors and play board games or share stories. With the families' permission, you could even "interview" some of the residents on video, encouraging them to talk about their childhood, their loved ones, and interesting events that they were a part of.

70 Volunteer at the Animal Shelter

Is your local animal shelter as overwhelmed and in need of help as many others across the country? If so, they may need help with administrative tasks, dog walking, or interacting in other ways with the sheltered animals. Just be sure that before you arrive you have already discussed and agreed upon whether you'll be taking any of the animals home. It's easy to fall in love with fur babies and hard to walk away!

71 The Very Thought of Thee . . .

How often do you think of your husband or wife throughout the day? If you kept a simple count of all the times he or she flashed through your mind throughout your busy day, you would probably be surprised. And maybe your spouse would be pleasantly surprised as well! This is one of those dates that will require your attention during the day, but the payoff will be well worth the extra time you spent.

Carry around with you a tiny notebook or piece of paper throughout the day. Every time you have a thought about your sweetie—*any* thought—make a hash mark on the paper. It could be as simple as "I have to remember to tell him that joke," or "Wow—my wife is beautiful. I'm a lucky man!" Start first thing in the morning, and continue until it's time for your evening together. Some of these thoughts will be quick flashes, and some of them will be lingering, but the important thing is to notice how often your spouse crosses your mind, and then to make sure that they know.

Before your date, pick up a bunch of flowers or chocolate kisses -whichever your sweetie will appreciate. There should be one "treat" for every hash mark on your paper. You can surprise your spouse at the door with the bouquet or chocolates all at once, or you can give out a few treats at a time throughout the evening. But at some point, give him or her a sweet card with the marked-up piece of paper inside. Let your husband or wife know that you think of them often throughout your day and you wanted them to know. This will be followed by an almost guaranteed "Aww . . . really?" and a hug from the one you've been thinking of all day. What a great way to start or end your evening together!

"If I had a flower for every time I thought of you,
I would walk in my garden forever."

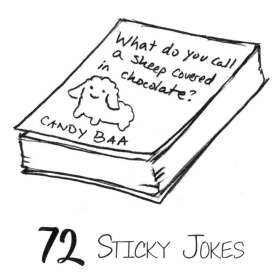

72 STICKY JOKES

Sometimes the best way to feel happy is to spread cheer! And when you make it a team sport, it's twice the fun. This whole date takes place at your local mall (or department store, if that's what you have to work with), but don't worry— your most costly investment will take place at the food court.

The Plan

Step One
Head over to the bookstore and pick up an inexpensive and cheesy joke book. While you are there, pick up pens and a couple of pads of brightly colored sticky notes.

Step Two

Go to the food court! You can't expect to carry out this project without the appropriate sustenance, right? While you are enjoying your pizza, burger, or taco, pull out your joke book, your sticky notes, and a couple of pens. Start writing jokes on your sticky notes—the more, the merrier. But keep the jokes clean! (Meaning no ketchup or soy sauce on the paper!)

Step Three

With sticky jokes in hand, head out into the crowd. Being as sneaky as possible, leaving one of your funny sticky notes in the food court somewhere in your view. Wait for someone to pick it up and get a little laugh. If they don't throw it away, be sure to do so. You don't want to leave any extra work for the mall employees. After that, move to another location and leave another joke for someone to find. Try to leave them anonymously if you can, and if you get to peek in on some of the reactions, that's even better. But wherever you leave them, be sure to go back and pick them all up. The idea is to spread some laughs - not a bunch of litter!

"I believe there is a direct correlation between love and laughter."

—*Yakov Smirnoff*

73 Happiness Rocks!

There is a wave of happiness rocking the nation, and wouldn't you like to be a part of it? This date will have you spreading brightly colored cheer all over town.

A "Happy Rock" is, well, a rock (surprise!) that is intended to make the finder feel loved, needed, and noticed. These rocks are being found on trails, in businesses, on front porches, in parks, and basically anywhere. When someone finds a happy rock, he or she can put it back where it was found, keep it, or hide it somewhere else for someone else to find. They are essentially smooth, colorfully painted rocks with words of encouragement, smiley faces, scriptures, or just symbols that make the creator and the finder of the rock feel happy. You get the picture, right?

What You Will Need

- Smooth, flat-ish rocks—They can be purchased to save time, or you can hunt for them in their natural place—near streams and rivers. (Make this a part of your date! Rock hunting!)
- Acrylic paint and paintbrushes—If you plan to write words on your rocks, paint pens will give you a little more control.
- A water-resistant sealant—A sponge-on sealer like Mod Podge will work, but it takes about twenty-four to forty-eight hours to dry completely. So if you were hoping to deliver your happy rocks on the same evening that you paint them, you might want to go with a spray varnish or fixative, such as Crystal Clear or something similar. Both types of sealant can be found at any arts and crafts store.

Now for the creative part. Cover your workspace to keep it clean, and gather your paint supplies. If you search online for "happy rocks," you will find a wide variety of examples to get your ideas flowing. Anything thoughts, images, words, or phrases that are positive and uplifting will work! So get your imagination and your expressive energy flowing.

Now it's time to spread some cheer! Who needs a little love? Who needs some cheering up? Who needs to be reminded that they matter?

Leave your rocks in some of these places:

- A hospital parking deck
- A veterans memorial
- A cemetery
- Outside the Department of Social Services
- A college campus
- A bus stop
- A neighbor's house
- A clinic or rehab center
- A police station
- A fire department

Sharing love with others will make love grow and blossom between the two of you.

Important Note

Be considerate about where you leave the rocks. Don't leave them where they might get run over by a lawn mower or a car. Don't leave them where someone might step on them. Don't leave them where small children may put them in their mouths.

74 HEART ATTACK

Do you have a coworker or friend who has been under a lot of stress lately? What about someone you see at church, or a neighbor? Don't forget about family members: a grandmother who has been under the weather, a dad who serves everyone except for himself, or a child that recently moved into his or her first apartment or dorm room and has eaten ramen noodles every night for the past week. When choosing someone to serve, you really can't go wrong. And nothing makes you feel the love more than sharing it!

The Plan

Gather the following items together ahead of time so you have plenty of time to get creative once your date starts:

- Construction paper—This will be for cutting out hearts, but don't limit yourself on the color. There are no rules that say hearts can only be red!

- Poster board—Make it big so it will hold lots of hearts, but not too big to fit on someone's door.
- Candy—Plenty of chocolates or miniature candy bars will work great.
- Tape, glue, or a stapler—Use these to attach the hearts and candy to the poster board and to hang the poster board on the door. Just make sure that the tape you choose won't pull the paint off the front door. (That would certainly ruin the surprise!)
- Markers or pens—Get creative with colors and write messages on the hearts.

Get to work! While one of you is cutting out hearts (don't worry about perfection!), the other one can be writing messages on them. You can use inspirational quotes, scripture verses, or simply write, "You're amazing!" or "You are loved!" Whatever will put a smile on their faces and warm their hearts. Be sure to leave about one-third to one-half of the hearts blank, and attach individual candies to those. In the middle of your poster board, write, "You've been heart attacked!" and then tape, staple, or glue your sweet messages all around. If you have some candies left over, you can fill a small gift bag to hang on their doorknob. Now you are ready to make your secret delivery!

This is the tricky part! No giggling allowed! Once you arrive at your secret destination, park your car a few doors down so your "victim" doesn't know you are coming. *Quietly* sneak up to the front door and hang your poster. If you have a clean getaway, go ahead and ring the doorbell. Then HIDE! If there is no way you could get away that quickly, then just leave it on the door, and they'll find it soon enough. Remember that keeping it a secret is the best part! It's not important for them to know who "attacked" them—only that they are loved and valued. And you will be creating a memory that only belongs to the two of you, making it even sweeter.

75 How Do I Love Thee? Let Me Count the Ways

Sometimes we need to recognize all the day-to-day things that our spouse does for us, both for our sake and for theirs! This date will take some preparation, but the rewards will last long after the date is over.

The Plan

On MONDAY

Pick up two tiny notebooks (nothing fancy—don't spend over a dollar on it!). You each will keep your notebook with you for the entire week and use it to record the things that your spouse does throughout the week that make your life better, happier, or just easier. Each day, try to write down at least a couple of things. In the beginning, you might have to make a special point to notice all the things your spouse does for you. But it should get easier throughout the week.

- Did you get an unexpected compliment this week?
- Did you get a phone call just to say hi?
- When you had a tough day at work, did your husband or wife listen sympathetically while you vented?
- Was your spouse especially patient with the kids this week?

On DATE NIGHT

At the end of the week, plan a nice, relaxing dinner (either at home or at a restaurant, whichever your budget allows) and pull out your tiny notebooks. Take turns sharing with your husband or wife all of the times you were grateful for them during the week. Take your time and don't rush it. Be sincere - with only uplifting and thankful comments. This is not the time to criticize; it is a time to show appreciation for the little things. You will be amazed at how far a little gratitude will go!

76 Random Acts of Kindness

Do you notice the homeless who stand on the street corners? Often when we are out and about, going through our hectic day, small acts of service come into our minds as we are rushing to and fro, but we usually aren't prepared to stop and act on the ideas we have.

On this date, you and your sweetie will be assembling your own "random acts of kindness" basket to keep in your car. Then, as you drive around town, you'll be looking for ways to make others smile. Here are some items to put in your basket:

- Multiple pairs of gloves (dollar stores often have pairs of gloves for $1–$2)
- Ten pairs of warm socks
- Scarves and hats
- Protein bars
- Individual bags of fruit snacks
- $1 bills
- Juice boxes or water bottles
- Anything else that might brighten the day of the homeless person you pass

After you have assembled your basket, take a drive around town and spread some cheer. Don't forget to replenish your basket as often as you can so you can keep the giving alive!

For an added touch to your date, pick up a bouquet of flowers and hand out a flower to random people on the street until you run out!

SNEAKY SPEEDY SERVICE PROJECTS

There is nothing more fun than being sneaky. And when you can work together to do a quick service for someone else, you make their day brighter and your time together more meaningful.

Here are four different date ideas that will likely be appropriate for all four seasons. Why not plan a "service date" for at least once a quarter? Each time, be sure to choose your target carefully, keeping in mind that the point is to remain anonymous and hidden so only you and your sweetie know of the good deed that was done. These clandestine projects can be done in the morning, afternoon, or evening, depending on when you can be at your stealthy best. And remember to take your own equipment.

77 Shoveling Snow

Shoveling snow in some parts of the country is a necessary evil and very strenuous work! Choose an elderly neighbor, a single mom, or a friend who could use a good deed, and sneak over when they are not home or are asleep. Work quickly and quietly, and then leave this note behind where they can see it:

Decided today to shovel your snow
Because you are loved more than you know.

78 RAKING LEAVES

Before your busy neighbor's house disappears behind the piles of leaves that he does not have the time to rake, sneak over and take care of the raking and bagging when no one is at home. Have fun, but be sure you know how much time you have to work with and when to expect him to return home. Be gone by the time he arrives, and leave only this note behind:

You are loved more than you believe,
So we decided to rake your leaves.

79 WASH YOUR FRIEND'S CAR

This one might be a little tricky and require some extra planning or an accomplice with keys to the family car! But imagine what a nice surprise it would be to climb into the minivan that usually smells like stale Cheerios and has sticky fingerprints on every surface only to find it shiny, gleaming, and smelling fresh and clean! Leave this note on the steering wheel and slip away, ninja style.

We decided today to wash your car
To show you are admired from afar.

80 MOW A LAWN

Do you know that family in the neighborhood that always takes a nice, long vacation in the summer only to come home to a neglected yard that resembles an African jungle? Or is there a family who had to leave town unexpectedly, and their lawn could use some TLC? This good deed will make you sweat, but it'll give you a feeling you won't forget! Leave this note behind:

We really missed you when you were gone;
To prove our love, we mowed your lawn!

PLAY TO WIN

When it comes to sports, the couple who plays together, stays together. Go Team Us!

81 SHOOTING HOOPS ONE ON ONE

Back in 1891, Dr. James Naismith had no idea that the game of throwing soccer balls into peach baskets would turn into the beloved sport of basketball. He also probably never imagined how romantic a game of one on one could be either!

Where to Go

The location for this date can be very versatile. Do you have access to a gym? What about a local park? They often have outdoor basketball courts. What about your driveway? If you have a hoop in your driveway, you don't even have to leave home to show your prowess on the court.

What to Wear

Dress in shorts and a T-shirt, and be sure to wear good sneakers with nonslip soles. You don't need a trip to the emergency room to impress your date.

The Plan

If you both know the rules pretty well, you can have fun playing a standard game of half-court one on one. You can add some interest by changing the rules up a little bit in the following ways:

- Left-handed shots only
- Make it—take it. (When you make a shot, you keep "the ball" until you miss.)
- Ball has to bounce (be dribbled) at least ten times before shooting
- All shots have to be outside the "key" (the "key" is the area from the goal to the half circle painted on the floor, behind the free-throw line. Shots "outside the key" are the longer, more difficult shots)

If you need something a little simpler and less strenuous, you may want to opt for a shooting game instead.

Around the World: Take turns shooting from designated spots around the court. If you make your shot, you keep shooting, but if you miss, you have two choices: you can either stay where you are and the next player starts shooting, or you can take another try at the same shot. If you miss it twice in a row, you go all they way back to the beginning. If you make it, you keep going. Whoever makes it "around the world" first wins.

H-O-R-S-E: This game is all about matching shots. You win by making shots that your opponent will likely miss. Player A shoots from anywhere on the court. If they miss their shot, the ball goes to Player B, who can shoot from anywhere. If Player A makes the shot, Player B has to duplicate the shot. If Player B misses the shot, then they are assigned the first letter (H), and play continues. The first person to be awarded all the letters of the word "HORSE" loses the game. But hold on a second . . . You can have some fun with this one! How about a friendly wager? If whoever loses has to provide the winner with a back rub, then spell out B-A-C-K-R-U-B. If the loser will have to wash the car, then missed shots should spell out C-A-R-W-A-S-H. How about M-I-L-K-S-H-A-K-E, or P-I-E?

You get the picture. If you want to add an element of intrigue to the game, then spell out M-Y-C-H-O-I-C-E, and at the end of the game, the winner gets to announce their prize.

The point here is to have fun and get a little exercise. So be a good sport, don't take the game too seriously, and don't forget to collect your prize at the end of the night. Give a basketball date a shot!

82 PAINTBALL

This date idea is definitely for the active and adventurous couple. Your adrenaline will be pumping so hard from running, jumping, climbing, and dodging paintballs that you won't even notice all of the calories you're burning! You'll easily find a paintball field in your area, but check their website to find out what kind of package you can get with all the paraphernalia that goes with it. (This can get a little pricey, but watch for coupons and deals to bring the cost down.) And keep in mind, this is not a dress-to-impress date. Wear pants and long sleeves to prevent battle wounds.

83 TAKE ME OUT TO THE BALLGAME

Put on your baseball hats, grab your pennants, and head to the ballpark! Baseball is America's national sport, and it's a perfect day or evening out for any couple! It really doesn't matter if you've never been to a game before or you are die-hard fans. With a little pre-game planning and research, you might even become crazed fans yourselves.

- Minor league baseball games are usually inexpensive, with tickets to fit any budget. They are even cheaper if you buy them in advance. But if your budget allows, by all means, hit the major leagues!
- Games are rarely canceled because of rain, heat, or cold, but they may be put on hold if a summer storm comes up, so be prepared for the weather in your area. Most fans bring rain gear or plastic ponchos along (they're cheap and fold up easily), and seat cushions are a good option if you become uncomfortable after sitting for long periods of time.
- Embrace the traditions! If this is your first time to a game, do some research beforehand on the teams and the stadium, and you'll find some fantastic baseball lore to entertain your date with before the game starts. Prepare to sing along to classics like "Take Me Out to the Ballgame" and Neil Diamond's "Sweet Caroline" during the seventh inning stretch. Don't be shy! You're here to create memories together.
- Concessions aren't cheap (especially at a major league stadium), so either eat before you come or make sure to have some cash on you if you want to buy food or drinks from the vendors. Hot dogs, corn dogs, and cracker jacks are a tradition!
- And be prepared—they usually have a jumbotron, where fans who are having the most fun (or kissing!) will be put on screen! Be prepared for that dramatic smooch if you get the chance to show your affection to your sweetheart in front of the whole crowd!

84 BOWLING

You'll laugh. You'll trash talk. You'll eat some fantastic comfort food. Bowling is such perfect date! It's active enough (if you play too many games in a row, you'll have a hard tome getting out of bed the next day), but there is plenty of time to eat and chat between turns.

Unless you're a pro bowler, you're probably going to make a few mistakes. Laugh them off. Laugh together. Nothing spices up a date like laughter and a healthy dose of silliness.

Bowling is moderately priced, depending on how many games you play and what time of day you are there. Check the website for half-price specials and other discount deals.

85 Tee for Two

Whether you are a golf pro with a great swing or you think that "PGA" stands for pre-game appetizers, going to a driving range is just *fun*. And whatever your level of expertise is, you'll either learn a new skill or have a friendly competition—but either way, you'll enjoy this time together.

How to Prepare

- Call ahead to find out if you need to reserve your time at the driving range.
- Do you have your own clubs? It is okay if you don't. Club rental is usually about $1 per club (and you only need one each).
- You can pay for a small basket of balls for each of you (around thirty-five balls), or you can share one jumbo basket (150–200 balls) for under $15 at most locations. There is no walking involved, so this date is not terribly physical. At a driving range, the idea is to improve your form and the distance and accuracy of your swing, so you just stand in one place and hit ball after ball.
- If you have never swung a golf club, it might be a good idea to watch a few videos ahead of time about proper form so you can enjoy yourself and stay injury-free.

Now that's an inexpensive and awesome date!

86 Miniature Golf

A game of mini golf is as a classic date night idea as it gets. Even if you snooze when the Golf Channel comes on, there's something about a miniature course, complete with clown hazards and six-foot-tall spinning windmills, that brings out the competitive nature in all of us. Whether you are young or old and whether you have any physical limitations, couples of all stages of marriage can enjoy playing mini golf together.

This date is all about having fun, so choosing your course is fairly unimportant. You may have the option of an eighteen-hole course over a nine-hole course to stretch the activity out, or you could take advantage of second-round discounts and play the course twice!

Have fun, but don't be afraid of a little competition. You could have a friendly wager, if you'd like to spice things up a bit. The loser gives the winner a foot massage or does the dishes for a week, whichever is more important to you!

Make this a double date if you know another couple that can have fun and be competitive at the same time. Grab some ice cream afterward!

87 "Friday Night Lights"

Friday-night football games never get old and are a great way to support your local community!

The Plan

Rah! Rah! Go team! In the fall, local high schools have football games on Friday nights that are exciting, inexpensive, and filled with school spirit!

Where should you go? Do you have connections with a local school, such as a grandchild who is a cheerleader, or a neighbor in the marching band? It's fun when you have someone's name to shout! But even if you don't know a single soul associated with the school, pick a side and cheer them on to victory!

Important Tips

- Check the weather, and dress for warmth! Pack a couple of blankets and seat cushions to make the bleachers more comfortable. Pick hats, scarves, and gloves in the school's colors.
- Check local schedules online or in the newspaper and plan to get there early for the best seats.
- Go to the game ready to make some noise! Buy a couple of team pompoms to help show your spirit. Remember that high-school football games are only partially about the game itself. They are social events, so be social! Enjoy the band, watch the halftime show, and eat the food!

Make It Fit

- For newlyweds—Sit behind the band and ask someone to give you a crash course in the school fight song, chants, and cheers. Draw upon your inner high schooler and sing along to the top of your lungs! Go team!
- For young parents—Enjoy the junk food! The kid's aren't watching, so take this opportunity to eat all the nachos, popcorn, and hot dogs you can handle.
- For empty nesters—Grab a game program on the way in, and take some time to look through the team rosters. Pick a player or a cheerleader to "adopt" for the night. Learn their name and jersey number, and cheer for them enthusiastically throughout the night. If you can, leave a small treat for them (from the concession stand) with a note saying, "Great game!"

A PARTY OF TWO

Food is comfort, food is fun, food is new
and exciting. Sharing those feelings with
the one you love doubles the flavor.

88 A GOOD MARRIAGE IS LIKE A CASSEROLE . . .

This double date will be sure to fill your belly with tasty comfort foods and fill
your evening with friendship, laughter, and a wee bit of competition. You'll
even leave with a new recipe to try at home.

So why is a good marriage like a casserole? There are three reasons, and
you'll explore all three on this date with your friends.

1. Like a good marriage, casseroles usually have many ingredients.
2. A good marriage is built in layers, like most casseroles.

3. The only ones who know what goes into a casserole (or a marriage) are the ones who are responsible for putting it together.

Both couples are responsible for making a casserole. The recipe is to remain secret until the end of the evening, but there are certain requirements:

*   Include at least five ingredients—salt and pepper are *not* ingredients!
*   You will eat your own casserole, so don't make it too crazy.
*   Have a spending limit that you are both comfortable with.
*   Bring the casserole pre-mixed and covered, but unbaked, to the house where you'll be dining (keep the ingredients secret!).

While your casseroles are baking, play a game or watch a movie to pass the time. When dinner is ready (you can add a salad and bread or other sides if you'd like), come together and discuss the following over your meal:

1. What are some of the ingredients that make your marriage a good one? Talking about your marriage's strengths is a great way to remember them and to learn from other couples.
2. Talk about some of the foundational layers on which your marriage is built. Examples could be faith, respect, kindness, and so on.
3. What are some things that your spouse does to make your marriage work that others might not be aware of? Is he or she incredibly patient and forgiving? Does he or she sacrifice happily? Is he or she your best friend? This is a great time to brag about your sweetheart in a comfortable setting.

How's dinner? Are you enjoying your casseroles? Can you figure out all of the ingredients? Pass out index cards and pens to each person at the table. Write down what you think is in the other couple's casserole. Once you've determined who came the closest to guessing all the ingredients, go ahead and exchange recipes!

Now you know why a good marriage is like a casserole! Dessert, anyone?

89 Apple Picking

Apple picking is the ultimate autumn date experience! The scenery is perfect, the air is crisp, and you get to be a hero when you bring home buckets of apples!

Where to Go

A quick search of PYO (pick your own) orchards will be a great starting point. A website that is particularly helpful is www.orangepippin.com/orchards. They list orchards by state with addresses, seasonal information, and fruit varieties that are available. Some orchards even have hayrides and gifts shops, so be sure and take advantage of the whole experience!

Dress warmly with comfortable shoes, and go at the right time. Early September to mid-October is the peak picking season in most of the United States.

Bring cash in small bills, if possible. Most family orchards don't accept credit cards and don't have a lot of change on hand.

Important Tips

Not all apples are created equal. Below is a quick guide to the best apple varieties for cooking, baking, and eating.

- **Fresh eating apples:** Pink Lady, Gala, Fuji, Honeycrisp, Red Delicious, McIntosh
- **Apple pie:** Cortland, Granny Smith, Braeburn, Golden Delicious, Pink Lady, Honeycrisp
- **Apple butter:** Cortland, Golden Delicious

- **Applesauce:** McIntosh, Cortland, Gravenstein, Golden Delicious, Jonagold
- **Apple cider:** Gala, Gravenstein

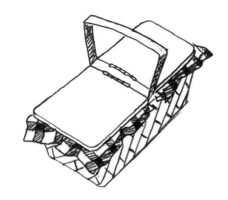

90 Backyard Picnic

Sharing a meal together outdoors surrounded by nature is delightful, but having a picnic in your own backyard affords you some comforts and conveniences that you won't have at the local park!

Top Ten Reasons to Picnic in Your Own Backyard

10. Shorter distance to carry the picnic basket
9. Less time to pay the babysitter (if you even need one at all!)
8. You don't need to bring a cooler. You have a fridge about 20 steps away.
7. No strangers
6. If you run out of cheese or crackers, just run in the kitchen and grab some more.
5. The dogs that are begging for your food are yours.
4. If it starts to rain, you can run inside and dry off.
3. With the help of an extension cord, you can watch a movie.
2. Privacy.

And the number one reason for picnicking in your backyard (drumroll, please!) . . .

1. No spiders in the restroom.

So make some sandwiches, grab a blanket, and enjoy a hassle-free time in your backyard together!

91 BERRY SWEET DATE

Berry picking is one of the simplest summer dates and also one of the most pleasurable! When you get home from the orchard, enjoy the fruits of your labor by making a batch of quick refrigerator jam.

When to Go

Throughout the United States, berry-picking season usually begins in June, when strawberries, blueberries, blackberries, raspberries, and even cranberries begin to appear, and ends in early August. Late morning, after the early morning dew has evaporated and before the hottest part of the day, is the ideal time to pick berries.

Where to Go

Berry picking is plentiful in most areas that have warm spring and summer months, so look online for "pick your own berries" orchards, and you'll find at least a few to choose from. Even if you have to take a short drive, fresh berries are worth the time!

How It's Done

Some orchards provide clean containers, but it might be a good idea to check on that before you go. You'll pay for your spoils by the pound or by the basket (only a few dollars), so make it worth your while and load up!

Bring cash in small bills; make sure you have protection from the sun, such as sunscreen and a hat; wear lightweight clothing, but preferably long pants to protect you from bugs and bees (yes, it's a farm!); and bring water to drink.

When you get back home (and cool off a bit), try your hand at making jam together. This refrigerated version is super easy and tastes yummy. (If you want to cut down on the sugar, you can, but you will have to boil the mixture a little bit longer.)

Freezer Jam

Ingredients

- 1 lb. fresh berries
- ¼ cup water
- 1 cup sugar
- large pinch salt
- 1 Tbsp. lemon juice

Directions

1. Wash the fruit and remove any stems. Roughly chop the fruit up into large chunks.
2. In a saucepan (at least two quarts in size) combine all of the ingredients over medium heat. Mash the fruit and sugar with a potato masher or a fork.
3. Bring the mixture to a boil and continue to cook over medium heat, stirring occasionally, for about twenty minutes, or until the juices thicken. It will become much thicker as the jam cools, so don't overcook it.
4. Let it cool completely, and then store your jam in an airtight container or jar in the refrigerator for up to three weeks, or in the freezer for up to four months.

92 BACKYARD CAMPFIRE DINNER

Do you remember those wonderful foil dinners you made as a kid in the campfire at summer camp? This dinner date will prove that campfire dinners are not just for scout camp anymore!

If you have a fire pit in your backyard, start by getting a fire going. If not, you can use your grill. While one if you is building and maintaining the fire, the other one should be building the foil dinner.

The Best Foil Dinner

Ingredients

- ½ medium onion, peeled and sliced
- ½ lb. lean ground beef
- 2 medium potatoes, peeled and sliced
- 2 medium carrots, peeled and sliced
- salt and pepper
- garlic salt
- seasoned salt
- butter (optional)

Directions

1. Lay out two sheets of 12-inch heavy-duty foil.
2. Place onion slices on the center of the foil, making a base for your hamburger patty to go.
3. Shape the ground beef into two hamburger patties.
4. Place the hamburger patties on top of the onions.
5. Add the sliced potatoes, and then add the carrots.
6. Add salt, pepper, garlic salt, and seasoned salt to taste.
7. Add butter if desired.
8. Fold the sides of the pouches to seal them.

Put the pouches on the hot coals in the fire, and relax with your date by the fire for 30 to 40 minutes, until the beef and vegetables are done. Tell campfire stories or ghost stories while you wait for your delicious dinner to cook. When you are finished with dinner, don't forget to roast marshmallows!

93 Convenience Store Dinner

We went to the Outer Banks in North Carolina on our honeymoon. One evening, we were trying to catch the last ferry to the more-populated island of Ocracoke before we stopped for the night. Unfortunately, the departure schedule we had wasn't accurate, and we missed our chance to make it onto the ferry. The island we were on wasn't very populated at all, and we ended up having to drive back several miles before we found a motel that had any vacancies. Vacancies were all it had. There was no phone in the room (this was before the days of cell phones), no alarm clock, and no TV. Needless to say, there were no restaurants anywhere nearby either, but there was a convenience store right next door. So we bought dinner from the convenience store and sat on the dock behind the little motel looking over the water inlet that evening. It was a very frustrating series of events that turned into a memorable, romantic dinner of Vienna sausages and corn sticks.

There are so many more options to making dinner than Vienna sausages and corn sticks, however. Your challenge, if you both choose to accept it, is to make a real dinner from ingredients purchased at a convenience store. One idea is refried beans, black olives, sour cream, cheddar cheese, rice, salsa, and tortilla chips to make nachos. Or you could both shop separately and see who can come up with the tastiest, most creative solution. Just be sure to check the dates on everything!

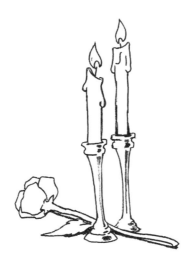

94 Candlelit Dinner for Two

Surprise your husband or wife with the ultimate romantic dinner. After you've cooked his or her favorite dinner (or after you've had it delivered), dress in your finest attire and invite your spouse into your "fine dining" room. Sit them at a lovely table complete with a tablecloth, fine china (not Chinet!), your best silverware, and lit candles. With soft music playing in the background and dim lights, answer their most pressing question, which is, "Why did you go to all this trouble?" Your response is simple: "You deserve it."

95 MEET AT A CAFE FOR LUNCH

If both you and your spouse have full-time jobs, it might be tough to feel romantic at the end of a long day. So why wait until the end of the day? Send a single flower to your sweetheart (by courier, if possible) with a note:

> *Meet me at* _____ (a favorite cafe) *for lunch at* _____ (whatever time works for you both).
>
> *Love,*
> _____ (sign your name)

Enjoying your lunch together will make the afternoon go a lot better!

96 TASTE OF THE TOWN

If you're not familiar with what a progressive dinner is, it's a dinner party spread out over several homes. Each person or couple invited hosts a portion of the dinner at their house. To make it more fun, the dinner can follow a theme, such as a holiday, sporting event, birthday, graduation, retirement, an Iron Chef challenge, and so on. It can be for any reason you get together with friends or family.

Each home is assigned a different course of the meal. Possibilities include an appetizer, a salad, an entree (sides are brought to the house responsible for the main course), and a dessert. Games, gift exchanges, movies, and so on can accompany each stop or can happen at the end, in the last house. The idea is to focus on everyone having fun. Nothing should be too stressful on any one household, and invitations can include voluntary course options.

There should be a set amount of time to be spent at each stop so that the evening doesn't stretch into the morning. There will be plenty of opportunities to lose track of time with the all of the visiting, eating, and gaming.

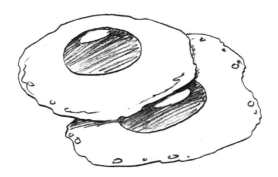

97 Over Easy, Please

Why don't we do more breakfast dating? It's less expensive than dinner, you're fresh off of a good night's sleep (hopefully), and you aren't bringing a day's worth of baggage with you to the conversation. What a great way to start the day!

Pick a restaurant. How hard can this be? You only need to decide two things:

1. How hungry are you? Do you need a breakfast buffet, or will you be satisfied with a glass of orange juice and a croissant?
2. How much time do you have? Are you going straight to a busy workday when you leave, or are you going home to do some early yard work and spend an afternoon watching ESPN or HGTV?

Beyond those decisions, breakfast food is breakfast food. Eggs, bacon, sausage, pancakes, biscuits and bagels . . . How many restaurants are there to choose from, really?

What will we talk about? Let's start with what you won't talk about: You won't talk about little Sally and Johnny fighting all day—again. You won't talk about the boss or about the co-worker who wants your job. You won't talk about getting the oil changed or forgetting the dry-cleaning.

Pick up a couple of newspapers, and talk about what's going on in the world. Share interesting headlines and articles with each other. By the time you get to your second plate of all-you-can-eat flapjacks, you'll have solved all the world's problems and will be ready to face the day together.

Well, maybe after a nap.

98 PICASSO AND PIZZA

At whatever your stage of marriage, trying something new together gives you a reason to laugh, brings out your humility, reminds you to pat each other on the back, and reminds you that sometimes the effort means everything. This date will give you an opportunity to try an art project together. And then, of course, your reward for being a good sport is in the form of pizza (talk about art)!

Pablo Picasso was one of the first artists to introduce the technique of "collage," which is defined by Merriam-Webster as "an artistic composition made of various materials (such as paper, cloth, or wood) glued on a surface."[1] He would use different materials, thoughtfully gathered and assembled, to create another shape or image. For example, he might cut images of models from a magazine, glue them down (overlapping), and form the silhouette of a female.

1. *Merriam-Webster Online*, s.v. "Collage," https://www.merriam-webster.com/dictionary/collage.

Here Is Your Art Project

On a large poster board, one of you will draw a simple outline of a house. No details—just the outline. Make it large but not bigger than a 16" × 20" outline. You can make it vertical or horizontal—whichever suits your fancy.

What You Will Need

- A 16" × 20" frame (you can get a poster frame for only a few dollars)
- 2 pairs of scissors
- Glue (white glue or a glue stick will do)
- Magazines, newspapers, fabric swatches, ribbon, etc.

Now the fun begins! Your goal together is to completely fill the house with words, images, colors, or symbols that you cut from magazines, newspapers, and so on that make your marriage and your home strong and loving. There should be no white spaces between the glued pieces. When you have filled the home with symbols of your love and commitment to each other and your family, cut the poster board to fit in your 16" × 20" frame. Hang it where you will see it and be reminded you of what you are working toward. If you are especially proud of your artistic skills, hang it where everyone can see it!

Now enjoy your pizza together. You've earned it!

99 Just Desserts

There is no need to spend time and money on a full three-course dinner every time you go out together. Haven't you ever wanted to skip dinner and go straight to dessert? Well, *shh*! The kids aren't looking—what are you waiting for?

A Selection of Excuses If You Feel You Need Them

"I worked late and I'm too exhausted for a long night out, but I still want to have a little catching-up time with my sweetie."

"We fed the kids the standard Wednesday-night chicken nuggets and mac-and-cheese dinner, and while washing the sippy cup for the twelfth time today, we spontaneously felt the need for some grown-up time together."

"I've been wanting to check out that hip, new cafe across town, but it also has a "hip" price tag, and an entire dinner at the hip cafe would cost us a week's salary."

"I am simply craving a cupcake from that cute little bakery downtown, but since we've implemented that strict no-sugar rule with the kids, it wouldn't be fair to have one in front of them . . . would it?"

"We have $9.41 in the bank account until payday, but the fast-food joint down the street has 99¢ ice cream sundaes."

A Little More Direction If You Need It

So now that you have picked the appropriate excuse to use, pick a place to go! A fast-food sundae or a slice of cheesecake at the jazz club downtown? What about a coffee shop that sells pastries and has free Wi-Fi? Or how about taking a deck of cards to that adorable old bakery that has tables for two?

Just get out of the house, have a sweet treat, and enjoy being a little irresponsible together! It's good for the soul and great for the marriage.

100 SECONDHAND RECIPE

The next time you and your spouse are asking the question, "What should we have for dinner?" try this interesting idea, and you might discover a whole new way of eating!

One of the reasons it's so fun to shop at thrift stores is that the low prices allow us to buy things that we normally wouldn't take a chance on. And there are so many unique and interesting things to see. Have you ever taken a look at the cookbooks that are sold at thrift stores? You can honestly find every strange, off-the-wall fad diet that ever existed since the invention of fire. Or pretty close to it.

For this date, take a ride to your favorite secondhand store, and peruse the cookbooks. Find the strangest one you can agree on, buy it, and pick a recipe to try for dinner. Then go to the grocery store and pick up the ingredients. It might be the "all raw" diet or the "all bacon" diet! Choose the one you'd both like to try and make it together.

Bon appétit!

101 MADE WITH L-O-V-E

No matter if you have been married one year or fifty years, all couples get into a kitchen-rut at some point during their relationship. In those times when you are bored with the same old dinners, it is tempting to pick up take-out or just go to a restaurant, but the easy way out can bust the budget! How about thinking outside the (pizza) box this time?

Go to the grocery store together, but instead of wandering aimlessly up and down the aisles waiting for an idea to jump out and grab you, play a little game. Tonight you will create a meal using ingredients that start with the letters, *L*, *O*, *V*, and *E*. The meal has to consist of one main dish, two sides, and a dessert. Do the words "liver," "lamb," or "lasagna" come to mind? What about "eggs" or "oranges?" "Veal," "venison," or "Vienna sausages?" Pretty much anything goes, but you have to agree to eat whatever your make!

Next time you get in a kitchen rut, think of another word or name to use as your shopping prompts and see what kind of scrumptious meal you can come up with!

AN ENTERTAINING EVENT

You don't always need to BE the main event.
Sometimes it's good to just relax and be entertained.

102 NIGHT AT THE IMPROV

Do you and your partner need a good belly laugh? On your next date, skip the pricey dinner (or eat at home before you leave) and put the cash into tickets for a comedy club instead.

Studies show that laughing gives our moods an instant lift and that those of us who do it most often tend to lead the happiest lives. Laughing together is a bonding experience, and the majority of women rate "a sense of humor" as the number-one thing they look for in a man. So wouldn't it stand to reason that a date that is all about laughing would be a great success?

Find a local comedy club or show online or in the newspaper. Make sure you reserve tickets ahead of time. Tickets to comedy shows are generally budget-friendly, except for when it comes to big-name comedians. However, it can be just as much fun (or even more) to pass on the big-name acts altogether and go to an open-mic comedy night or an improv event at a local comedy club.

Seats aren't assigned with your tickets, so arrive early to choose your seats. But be advised that the people closest to the front are often the ones picked on by the comedian!

This date might be even more fun if you bring along another couple and make it a double date! The more, the funnier!

"Laughter is the shortest distance between two people."

—*Victor Borge*

103 Tour an Art Museum

Art museums are full of priceless ancient pieces of art, and whether you and your spouse are into Monet, Renoir, Picasso, Georgia O'Keeffe, or none of the above, your afternoon strolling through the corridors of an art museum will be educational at least and fascinating at best!

Most state-sponsored art museums are publicly funded, so they are free to enter, but inside you will likely find exhibits from artists that you've only read about in history books. Do some research ahead of time to know if there are any special traveling exhibitions that you might want to check out, and plan your trip accordingly. If you miss the special traveling works, don't worry. The museum's permanent collection will probably be enough to wake up the tiniest spark of interest in art or history that the average adult has flickering within.

Prepare ahead to get the most out of your experience. Search the museum's website and read up on the art they have in house. Is there a particular painting that you are interested in seeing up close and personal? What about an artist that you'd like to learn more about? You will enjoy the experience much more if you have done a little homework in advance of your date.

When you arrive, pick up a printed map or brochure with the layout of the museum and the exhibits. You could easily spend a couple of days wandering through the halls of a large museum and still never see all the paintings, but if you know there is an area you have an interest in, go there first, and then decide how much more culture you want to soak up in one day.

It's okay to talk. If you have questions, ask! The guides are there to assist you, and they will know interesting facts about the artists and the art that may not be printed in your brochure.

If you have opinions, share! You are there with your sweetheart to have an experience together. If you like a style, say so. If you don't care so much for an artist, say so. If you aren't sure what a painting is trying to say to you, discuss it. The wonderful thing about art is that it is so subjective. You and your spouse will see totally different things in a painting, and when you talk about your thoughts and opinions, you'll learn from each other and you'll learn about each other.

Talk about color, composition, and value. Talk about how the painting makes you feel. Talk about what the painting reminds you of and what you think the artist was trying to convey. Talk about how much you love to spend time together.

Dress for the occasion. Aim for business casual, but dress comfortably as well. There is no need to dress in formal wear, unless you are going to an opening or closing exhibit reception. Wear shoes that are comfortable to walk in, but don't be afraid to make use of the many chairs and benches throughout the museum. Taking a rest will give you valuable time to ponder and quietly discuss the beautiful work you have seen.

104 B-I-N-G-O!

No need to be a senior citizen for this entertaining night at the bingo hall together! Cheesy? Maybe. But also cheap, unique, and possibly lucrative! It could be one of the liveliest dates you'll ever go on! Forget any preconceived ideas and you'll have a blast!

Wherever you are in the world, you're probably closer than you think to a friendly (or feisty) neighborhood bingo game. It can be a real test of speed and mental agility with some bingo veterans playing as many as thirty cards at a time! Entry fees are minimal, winnings can range from cash to electronics to furniture, and the people-watching opportunity is matchless!

Find a bingo game to join. While fewer in number than they used to be, plenty of bingo halls are still operating around the country. Beyond that, many churches, community halls, and veterans associations also host weekly games that attract regulars from miles around. If you don't know of any in your area, look online.

What to Bring

- Cash—to pay your entry fee and purchase snacks and drinks.
- Daubers—a special type of pen used to mark paper bingo cards. Regulars usually bring their own, but they can be purchased on site as well.
- Good-luck charms—optional, of course!

Important Tips

- All you really need is cash! Buy as many cards as you think you can each keep track of at once, but keep in mind that numbers are called very quickly, and the game will become more frustrating than fun if you keep falling behind. It might even be a good idea to watch a few rounds before you join in, so you know how things flow—but don't sit on the sidelines all night!

- The letters and numbers are called completely at random, so unless you are a super lucky person, don't expect to win anything. But do take the time to observe your neighbors (especially their wacky charms and superstitions) and have a friendly chat. You might make some new friends and decide to show up the following week!

105 Back to School

If you are looking for a engaging (and perhaps educational) evening on a budget, check out the nearest college campus for free or inexpensive public events! You'll feel like a kid again as you stroll hand in hand across the quad and stop in the campus cafe for dessert and a hot beverage.

What types of date-worthy events will you find on a college campus?

Art Exhibits

Colleges often host community art exhibits and competitions. If you are considering attending an art exhibit, it might be helpful to know if the event you are attending is "juried" or "non-juried." A juried show will exhibit the work of more accomplished, serious artists since they likely had to pay an entry fee and had more strict guidelines on size, medium, and genre. These exhibits are judged by qualified critics, art professors, and artists, and winners are awarded cash and other prizes.

If the event is "non-juried," then there are no judges and no awards, and anyone can enter anything in the show. These are very interesting with no restrictions on the genre or media, but be warned—truly anything goes.

Art exhibits are usually up for several weeks and you can browse them at any time, but if you attend the opening or closing reception, they will usually serve food and beverages, and you can meet the artists. It's also fun to be present when the awards are announced in a juried show.

Concerts

Check the campus events calendar for upcoming concert dates. Most of the bands and performers will be either local or start-ups, but you might be surprised at some of the big names that will offer a show on a college campus. Even if it's a no-name performer, you'll enjoy the atmosphere of being on campus again! The tickets might be full price for non-students, so check that in advance.

Lectures

Colleges and universities have lectures on campus about current events, political issues, social issues, and just about every topic you can imagine. You might have the opportunity to hear an author discuss his or her latest book or an elected official talk about policy debates or upcoming legislation. You might even hear a celebrity speak on an issue that he or she is passionate about.

Sporting Events

Depending on what sport you are hoping to see and which division the college or university plays in, ticket prices for well-known sports, such as football, basketball, soccer, or baseball, will vary. But some of the lesser-known teams will be more eager to fill seats, so ticket prices will be less expensive. Whether you are watching a football game with twenty-five thousand people or a women's volleyball game with one hundred people, live sporting events are impossible to sit still during, and you'll come away with a few new chants as well!

People-watching

Let's be honest—sitting on a bench in the quad and watching students in their element is entertainment at its finest. Take some time to share funny college stories of your own with each other, but beware—if you sit there too long and appear to be having too much fun, you might get invited to a frat party later that night!

106 Monumental Afternoon

Every city and town has a history, and usually that history is documented somewhere. Exploring local historical monuments and locations can make for a very entertaining date. So where do you start?

There are many ways to search your area. Here are some places you can start with:

- The National Parks Service website, where you can find the National Historic Landmarks Program. On this page, you can search by state for landmarks that have made it to the National Registry. But don't stop there!
- The historical society website for your state—most states have them.
- Apps for your phone that will help you track sites close to you.

Even if you are not a history buff, it is practically guaranteed that you will find something of interest in your area.

- Battlefields
- Historic buildings, homes, and businesses
- Landmarks where historical events took place

Spending time together discovering the history around you is a great way to bring more meaning to the here and now.

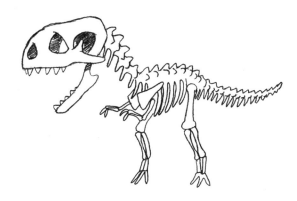

107 Night at the Museum

For an adventure into the wonders of science, visit a natural science museum together! This date will cost you very little, but you will take away shared knowledge of something new, and that is priceless!

Where to Go

Search online for science museums around you. Larger cities will have the most to offer, but don't ignore the smaller towns around you. The science museums in less metropolitan areas will be less expensive, but they may offer everything you are searching for. So what *are* you searching for?

What to Do or See

- Historical exhibits (cavemen, dinosaurs, prehistoric archeology),
- Live animal exhibits (reptiles, petting zoos, aquariums, insects)
- Movies (some have 3D theaters)
- Geography exhibits (rocks, gem, minerals)
- Dioramas, self-guided tours, and interactive experiences
- Special short-term, traveling exhibits and events (check the website for these)

How Much It Will Cost

Prices vary greatly depending on what part of the country you are in and what exhibits you are seeing. Some museums will have a general admission price that will get you into everything, and others will offer *a la carte* pricing so you can be a little choosier. There are some that will have a nice cafe to dine in, and almost all of them have a gift shop to purchase a little reminder of your experience. Plan your funds accordingly.

When to Go

You can call the museum to see when their busiest times are—so you can avoid them, of course. But if you do have to stand in line for an exhibit here and there, just take it in stride and use the time for some handholding and chit-chatting. Plan to spend about three hours investigating all your natural science museum has to offer.

108 Pajama-Wearing, Binge-Watching, Sofa-Snuggling, Ice-Cream-Eating, Staying-In Kind of Night

If your bank balance is looking a little sad and you're between paychecks, you can still have a great evening together! You just have to choose to be in the moment, with no distractions. You have a TV, don't you? Or a computer? What about a phone? Technology has made us so connected that finding a favorite TV show, movie, or documentary is as close as our fingertips and as cheap as a $7.99 monthly subscription! So what have you and your sweetheart been dying to see?

The key to this date is to be comfortable, relaxed, and snuggled up on the sofa together, and to let yourself get caught up in someone else's life!

What to Watch

Is there a sitcom that you keep hearing about at work or on social media? Are you more the reality-show type? Could you spend all night watching music or dancing competitions? Is there a historical documentary series that you could really sink your teeth into?

One of the best parts about binge-watching a TV series is that you can start from the very beginning, and you don't have to come in mid-season and try to figure out the drama and the story line! So here we go: season one, episode one.

WAIT! HOLD EVERYTHING! Where's the Ice Cream?

Okay, now you may begin. Season one, episode one . . .

You might want to put a time limit on this date (and force yourself to stick to it!) or else you'll be halfway through season six when the kids wake up for school!

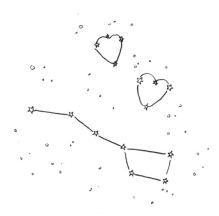

109 BOLDLY GO WHERE NO COUPLE HAS GONE BEFORE

Explore the night sky together at a planetarium or observatory. With expert guidance from an astronomy guide, you'll learn how to identify the planets, stars, and constellations. You'll also hear stories, legends, and other astronomical phenomena tailored to the season and your region.

Many planetariums also have holiday-themed star shows around Halloween, Christmas, and Valentine's Day. These events are generally educational, well produced, and inexpensive. There will also be free exhibits to enjoy, so be sure to allow time before or after your scheduled show to take advantage of everything that is offered. You will not be disappointed!

Shows usually cost around $10 per person and last about an hour. Reservations are recommended.

110 We Love a Parade!

No matter how old you get, there is something about the sights, sounds, and even smells of a parade that take you back to the giddiness of childhood. And the good news is that it is never hard to find one if you know how to look!

- Small towns—Small towns sometimes have big festivals, and festivals often start or end with a parade.
- Holidays—Thanksgiving, Christmas, and Independence Day are commonly celebrated with a parade, no matter where you may live.
- Military and honor—If you live near a military base or military school, you have an opportunity to see some awesome parades. But don't forget Veteran's Day and Memorial Day, when we honor fallen troops.
- Special occasion—If your sports team wins the national championship, or if a hometown hero comes home again, there might be a parade in celebration.

Make Your Day a Success

- Arrive early to get a good spot.
- Take a camp chair or something to sit on.
- Wear sunscreen, even if it's chilly.
- Take a hat and a lightweight poncho if there is a threat of rain.
- Wear comfy shoes—you'll likely have to park far away.

Enjoy waving at the participants and clapping with the marching bands. Whatever your parade is meant to celebrate, make it count!

111 Get Your Comic On

With the popularity of Comic-Con growing every year, to the casual onlooker, this event featuring fans dressing in extremely elaborate handmade costumes emulating their favorite characters from pop culture may seem bizarre. However, the science fiction convention has an extraordinarily long history. Since the 1930s, these conventions have drawn fans, a couple dozen to a couple hundred at first, from all parts of the world.

Depending on which convention you attend, the price varies widely. There are many small, local conventions that are much more cost effective. The larger events are more affordable when purchasing tickets for a single day and can be well worth the time and expense. It's an experience that won't be soon forgotten.

A couple of very thorough websites list just about every convention broken down into categories of genre, location, and date.

- fancons.com/events
- www.upcomingcons.com

Below are some of the more popular convention genres and a brief explanation of each.

Comic-Book Conventions

These events focus primarily on American comic books. Some regional comic cons are smaller, single-day conventions and focus on selling and trading comics. Larger events, lasting for almost a week, have more of a focus on meeting guest authors and artists as well as learning about new, upcoming projects.

Science Fiction Conventions

Sci-fi conventions traditionally have centered on science-fiction books and literature. They've expanded their focus to a variety of media, including gaming, movies, and TV. Most contain common components, such as actors, authors, artists, and publishers participating in autograph signings, Q&A panels, and discussions.

Gaming Conventions

Gaming conventions are events where gaming fans participate in various types of games, with a focus on video games, tournaments, and pen-and-paper roleplaying games, with producers and game developers attending to show off their latest products.

Literature Conventions

Book conventions feature reading, writing, and literature as key subjects. These conventions often feature author readings, discussions, writing seminars, and more.

Horror Conventions

Horror cons focus on the darker side of fantasy—many spotlight film festivals are devoted to screening new horror movies.

Anime Conventions

Anime cons are growing rapidly in popularity. There are dozens of anime conventions around the world, so it will be easy to find an anime convention near you.

The environment in any of these conventions is infectious. So strap on your phaser, grab your light saber, dive in head first, and have a blast!

112 SATURDAY MATINEE

Many theaters have special weekend matinees that aren't offered at their main showing times. Sometimes they are older movies or silent films. You might find a John Wayne or Elvis marathon, but whatever you show up for, the price will be much lower than a prime-time new release, the theater won't be as crowded, and when you come out of the movie theater, it will still be daytime!

Try a midday getaway by seeing a matinee together!

113 IT'S NOT OVER UNTIL . . .

Maybe you are a seasoned opera lover. Or perhaps you are just thinking about trying out a new music genre. Either way, everyone should attend the opera at least once. It can be surprisingly emotional and even romantic if you prepare in advance. At the very least, this will be a forever memory.

Do your homework. Most opera houses will post a synopsis of the operatic plot on their website so that you can take your time and read through it before you come for the performance. Operas are not typically in English, and even when they are, the words are hard to understand. So you will get much more out of the opera if you understand the story line in advance.

Get there on time. Most opera centers are in metropolitan areas, so be prepared for the traffic and plan to arrive earlier than you think you need to. If you get there after the curtain rises, you will not be allowed inside until there is a break. So don't be late.

Choose your seats carefully. Ticket prices vary greatly based on where you are sitting and what city you are in. Many seats (especially on the sides) will not have a full view of the stage, so understand that you get what you pay for.

The opera is a classy affair, so dress to impress. Opening and weekend night performances are usually the dressiest nights, where men will be in suits and women will wear nice dresses. Weekday and matinee performances are generally where you'll see opera-goers in business casual clothing. Be sure to pay attention to how long your show is going to be. An opera can last anywhere from an hour to four hours. Plan your evening and your attire accordingly.

Enjoy the opera!

114 Tall-Tale Tellers

Put away the cell phone, turn off the TV, and close the laptop. No technology is needed to have the time of your life at a storytelling festival. If you've never seen one of these professional "tellers" spin their tales, here is what to expect at a festival.

A storytelling festival is an event that features local, regional, and/or nationally known oral storytellers. Each storyteller has a scheduled amount of time to share a story with the audience, and the topic or their tale might include folklore, comedy, inspiration, drama, ghost stories, and more. The featured storytellers are often professional performing artists, but a festival allows opportunities for semi-professional or amateur storytellers to be included among the events. Every accent imaginable will be heard as participants travel from literally all over the world to tell their stories and compete for prizes.

These gatherings are held all over the country, some over many days with a packed schedule of events and thousands of tellers and listeners alike. Others are more intimate but no less entertaining.

Most events are free, although there may be a charge for workshops and the grand finale performance.

115 Pac Man and Space Invaders

It's true that smart phones and home entertainment systems have replaced the traditional arcade. They began shutting down by the later half of the '80s. The convenience of having your favorite games move from the local convenience store to the palm of your hand has been historic. However, many of us have fond memories of wasting hours (and quarters) at the boardwalk or shopping mall, slipping quarter after quarter into the glowing, dimensional transporters we called video games. There is something about the atmosphere found in an arcade that at-home gaming systems can't replicate.

Important Tips

To be honest, both partners in a marriage may not be video-game enthusiasts. Hang with me for a moment while we go over some technical information. Research[1] has shown that certain pathways in the forebrain are activated while playing video games. These are the brain's pleasure pathways, where dopamine is the neurotransmitter. A study by neuroscientist Marc Palaus in 2017 stated that gaming stimulates the cognitive portions of the brain that the game being played focuses on—games involving spatial memory, visual acuity, navigation, attention, and so on promote those areas in the brain. So if you aren't a fan of video games, unlike your spouse, suspend your preconceived prejudices against video games, jump in with both feet, and have fun in spite of yourself!

For this to be a positive experience, there needs to be mutual investment in the experience. It won't work for one person to play while the other stands by, even if cheering them on. There are many two-player games where the players are on the same side, working together to overcome a common obstacle. Enduring and conquering the adversity together will unify you while you're having fun together. While playing, focus on remaining positive, looking for solutions together, and supporting one another.

Two rolls of quarters can be a great way to not only strengthen your marriage, but to have an exciting adventure in the process!

1. Strenziok, M., Parasuraman, R., Clarke, E., Cisler, D. S., Thompson, J. C., and Greenwood, P. M. (2014). Neurocognitive enhancement in older adults: comparison of three cognitive training tasks to test a hypothesis of training transfer in brain connectivity. Neuroimage 85(Pt 3), 1027–1039. doi: 10.1016/j.neuroimage.2013.07.069.
2. Gong, D., He, H., Liu, D., Ma, W., Dong, L., Luo, C., et al. (2015). Enhanced functional connectivity and increased gray matter volume of insula related to action video game playing. Sci. Rep. 5:9763. doi: 10.1038/srep09763.
3. Hum. Neurosci., 22 May 2017.

116 THE WILD BLUE YONDER

There is nothing as exhilarating as a military air show! The loops, stunts, and tight formations will keep you in awe while an F16 fighter jet flying overhead will curl your toes and put butterflies in your stomach. It is truly a date for the record books, and you will love *ooh*ing and *ahh*ing together as you take in the sights, sounds, and smells associated with the sheer awesome power of military aircrafts.

Important Tips

- Go early! Arrive before the gates open.
- Check the website in advance to make sure you are allowed to carry in things like chairs, coolers, and backpacks. You are going to want something to sit on, and you'll be sitting in the sun with no shade, so bring hats, sunscreen, and plenty of water and snacks.
- When the planes fly overhead, you'll be looking straight up, so bring sunglasses.

- If there are shuttle buses to take you to the airfield from the parking area, take advantage of this service. Otherwise it is a very long walk.

Once you are in the gate, you will see different types of military equipment, and there will be servicemen there to talk about what they are and how they are used. There will be military planes that you can walk through, and sometimes you are allowed to even go into the cockpit.

117 TRIPLE TOE LOOP . . . WAIT, WHAT?

Going to a figure-skating competition is so exciting, and it's not an activity that most couples think to look for. This date will leave you with nothing but warm fuzzies for each other and for and the beautiful sport of figure skating!

How Much It Will Cost

While national- or world-championship events can run into the hundreds or even thousands per ticket, there are local, amateur, and adult skating competitions, which are much more reasonable.

What to Bring

- A good camera, if you want pictures (Because of the lighting, constant movement, and reflections off of the ice, a sub-par camera will be nothing but dead weight to keep up with.)
- Stuffed animals or flowers to toss down to the skaters after a great performance
- A seat cushion, if your seats are on bleachers or folding stadium seats (You'll be sitting a *lot*.)
- A cheerful attitude and lots of support for the skaters

At the Event

Try to cheer for everyone—especially the lower-ranked skaters. They don't get many opportunities to skate for a decent-sized audience, and they will appreciate the support.

Don't be shy. Most skating fans are friendly and will be happy to chat with another fan, but don't strike up a conversation during the performance. You won't make any friends that way.

Feel free to take pictures. The better times to take pics if you have a non-professional camera are when the skaters hit their opening and closing poses and when they take their bows—but NEVER use flash. Ever.

Ask for autographs and pictures after performances. If you feel comfortable asking, you should totally go for it. Skaters are usually gracious, and many are quite friendly with fans, so you'll have great souvenirs.

Stay standing at the top of your section, if you're coming back from the bathroom or concession stands until after the skater on the ice (if there is one) has finished his or her program. You don't want to distract the skater or be rude to the other spectators.

Check on the rink's re-entry policy. You may need to leave the facility to eat between events. Some rinks have a "no re-entry without stamp" policy, and it's good to know what it is before you leave and then can't get back in.

What to Wear

Dress in comfortable layers. Some rinks are colder than others, and the temperature will vary according to whether the rink is full of spectators or empty. Layering allows you to take off or add layers depending on those temperature variations.

118 Dinner and a Movie

Sometimes it's not about how creative you can be with an idea for a date. Sometimes a date can be a very simple, time-tested formula to de-stress. Because sometimes all you really need to do is relax with each other. Allow yourself some time to forget about the speed bumps in front of you and how you're going to get over or around them successfully. Below are some additional items to add to your simple solution date.

- Have a banana—Potassium can help increase your energy levels during times of stress.
- Get lost in a movie—Pick a good movie that will really suck you in, and allow yourself to get absorbed into it.

- Go for a walk—Just a ten- to fifteen-minute walk can really clear the cobwebs or regenerate your stressed-out batteries.

Seriously, de-stressing will help you bond and communicate with your spouse on a deeper level. It will also help you have a clearer, sharper mind when it's time to get back to solving those stressful situations. So take some time to focus on each other . . . You know, the things that *really* matter.

119 Dinner Theater

A scrumptious meal followed by a top-notch show is a memorable way for a couple of lovebirds to spend an evening together. Check out a dinner theater for a noteworthy date night!

This form of entertainment has been around for decades, and after your first experience, you'll understand why. A quick internet search will help you locate a dinner theater near you, and if there isn't one in your town, it's definitely worth the drive. The venue's website will give you all the information you need to plan your evening:

Dinner/show times: Often you will be asked *not* to arrive before your scheduled seating time. Check with your theater to know when to arrive. Plan to spend about three to four hours for dinner and the show.

Seating chart: Choose how close to the stage you want to be and how many others you want to share a table with.

Dress code: Usually business casual is appropriate, but special events may differ.

Pricing: Several factors can affect the price, including where you sit, what show you are seeing, and seasonal rates. Check for senior rates, matinee shows, and early-bird pricing to save a little cash. Tickets are often non-refundable, so be sure to check the theater's cancellation policy.

Menu: Some theaters have a full buffet while others have plated meals. If you have food allergies or other dietary restrictions, make that known at the time of the reservation.

Once you attend your first dinner theater, you'll want to return again and again!

HITTING ALL THE RIGHT NOTES

Music can create romance, fun, silliness, energy, motivation—but it always creates memories.

120 CHILDREN'S DANCE RECITAL

A children's dance recital is one of the best forms of entertainment around—and no, you don't have to have a child in the show to have a delightful time! As a matter of fact, you'll probably enjoy the show more without the stress of having your own child perform. Now, if you go expecting the New York City Ballet, then you will be slightly disappointed. (You aren't paying for the NYC Ballet, either!) But if you can sit back and enjoy the costumes, the set design, and the hard work of the small but dedicated students, then you will have a fabulous time. And it helps to have a sense of humor. Who knows—you might be watching a future member of the NYC Ballet!

121 THE SYMPHONY

If you've never attended the symphony, it's time you give it a try! Check the concert schedule ahead of time to choose the type of show you'd be most interested in. You might hear Broadway show tunes, patriotic music by Sousa, or even popular sounds like Paul McCartney. If classical is your thing, you will have many choices in that genre as well. Concerts last anywhere from one to two hours, and ticket prices start at approximately $30. Dress code is business casual to dressy.

122 OPEN-MIC NIGHT

The open-mic night is a tradition in the live music community of coffee shops and bars (around college campuses, mostly), and for a lot of musicians it is their first foray into performance. Often the mic is open to amateur performers one night a week to showcase their song writing, vocals, comedy, poetry, or dramatic reading. Check ahead to find out what night is designated as open mic, and give it a try.

123 HIGH SCHOOL MUSICAL

A great way to support your local community and see a pretty great show is to attend a high-school musical. Most schools put on an annual musical or play, and if your city has a high school that is focused on the arts, you might have even more opportunities to take in a performance. Tickets are inexpensive, and you can be sure that your money is going to a good cause!

Check out your local high school's website to find out when the upcoming performances are, and be sure to put them on your calendar if they are later in the year. Most schools don't have a very large auditorium, and performances might sell out if you wait until the last minute.

Why do actors act and dancers dance? For the audience, of course. So if you are particularly impressed by some of the performers, hang around after the show and tell them so! The cast usually heads for the lobby after the curtain call to take pictures and meet up with friends and family, so you might even have the opportunity to shake the hand and get the autograph of some budding talent or future celebrity.

One Step Further

After the show, if you are impressed by what you've seen, be sure to send an email to the school administrator and the county school board. Arts funding is always in danger of being cut, and it might help to hear from members of the community. Enjoy the show!

124 MUSIC IN THE PARK

There's nothing like an outdoor venue and live music, especially when it's free! This is a relaxing date that will take you out of your stress-filled life for a few hours to enjoy some nature, tunes, and most of all, great company!

Where to Go

Once the weather is comfortable for sitting outdoors, small towns and suburbia usually offer live music in the park. Your town should have an events calendar online that will possibly even tell you the name of the band performing and/ or the genre of music. Do you intend to sit back and listen, or are you the couple that will cut a rug as soon as the beat picks up? Do you prefer classical symphony? Or pop cover tunes? Keep all this in mind when you are choosing your location.

What to Bring

Frequently there will be food trucks or venders selling anything from pop-corn and candy to a gourmet dinner. So either eat before you go, or plan to dine on the park fare, but either way bring a little cash in case they aren't set up to take cards. Check with the park or town office ahead of time about bringing in drinks or coolers. Sometimes there are restrictions on what you can haul in.

Definitely take a blanket or some lightweight chairs for sitting on, and if you go in the afternoon, bring hats, sunglasses, and sunscreen. Possibly even bring a small umbrella to hide from the sun, but be mindful of the other con-certgoers around you.

Whatever happens, just go with the flow. This date is all about relaxing. So the band turns out to be terrible? Clap anyway! So no one else is dancing? Dance anyway! Take this time to enjoy your time together and leave the cares of the world out there, on the freeway. You'll be so glad you did.

125 I Write the Songs . . .

It's time to put on your creative hat for this date! Don't worry—absolutely no talent is necessary for this musical project. Just have an open mind and a will-ing heart, and you'll be amazed at what you come up with!

Do re mi fa sol la ti . . . GO.

Choose a song that you are both very familiar with. It's helpful if you at least know the melody and the chorus by heart. Search on the internet for an instrumental version of this song, and get out your pencil and paper.

The object of this date is to create an anthem or a musical tribute to your lives together. The most important thing is that you collaborate and create something you are both happy with. You can keep the chorus as is, if you need or want to. Some things to think about:

- Are you going to be singing to each other in a duet?
- Are you singing together about your relationship?
- Will it be silly or serious? Romantic or flirty? Fast or slow?
- Are you each going to write a verse alone, or will you work on the whole song together?

Here are some suggested songs to use as a backdrop—but use what you both like. Are you a fan of country music? Rap music? Make it all about you and your style together.

- "Let's Stay Together" by Al Green
- "Happy Together" by the Turtles
- "Monday, Monday" by the Mamas and the Papas
- Anything by Elvis
- Any Disney song

Once you have finished creating your masterpiece, don't forget to write it down and save it! And every time you hear "your song" on the radio, sing along with your new words!

126 Silly Love Songs

Lets face it—there are going to be weeks here and there when you just can't work out a night to be together. Maybe one of you is traveling or having to work late. This is no reason to lose your connection to each other!

No matter how long you have been married, you will have songs that are special and meaningful to you both. All you need for this long-distance date are two things: a smart phone and a little thoughtfulness.

How It Works

Think of a song that reminds you of your sweetheart, and then search for it on your phone using a music app or your phone's internet browser. Copy the link to the song and text it to your spouse. That's it. Now it's their turn. Don't worry if you can't think of many songs in the beginning. The longer you play the game, the more songs you'll be reminded of. Be funny, be sentimental, be romantic, but most importantly, just be connected. Let the game go on as long as the two of you can stay awake, but be prepared—it might go on for a few days.

Here are suggestions to get you started (You can always send the lyrics along with the song!):

- "You're the Best Thing That Ever Happened to Me"—Gladys Knight and the Pips
- "Sugar"—Maroon 5
- "Light Up"—Mutemath
- "Groovy Kind of Love"—Phil Collins
- "In Your Eyes"—Peter Gabriel
- "Silly Love Songs"—Paul McCartney and Wings
- "Teddy Bear"—Elvis Presley
- "Tear in My Heart"—Twenty One Pilots
- "Love is All You Need"—The Beatles
- "Just the Way You Are"—Billy Joel
- "Best of My Love"—The Emotions
- "I Got You Babe"—Sonny & Cher
- "Biggest Part of Me"—Ambrosia
- "Where You Lead"—Carole King
- "Beautiful"—Gordon Lightfoot
- "Ain't No Woman like the One I've Got"—The Four Tops
- "My Girl"—The Temptations

DATING 101

Some of the most meaningful memories occur
when you are learning and growing together.

One of the best ways to nurture your marriage through dating is to grow closer by growing together! Opportunities to learn a new skill, develop a new talent, or just learn about something you've always been interested in are everywhere. Look for some of the following classes at community colleges, home-improvement stores, libraries, craft stores, church groups, and local businesses. Some of them will be a one-time event, and some might take one night a week for a few weeks, but whichever you choose, remember that this is an opportunity for both of you to work together, help each other, and spend time with each other.

127 BALLROOM DANCE CLASS

Dancing can be a great way to keep the magic in your relationship or to bring it back if you lost it somewhere between changing diapers and paying college tuition. It's a way for the two of you to connect with each other and get away from chores, children, jobs, and the stresses in your lives. Dancing together forces you to touch each other, look at each other, and even breathe together.

Important Tips

Going to your very first ballroom dance lesson can be incredibly intimidating. You may be thinking *What if I look silly? What if I can't keep up?* or *What if I fall on my face?* No need to fear! Here are some things to know before you go.

What to wear: Wear something comfortable and easy to move in but not too sloppy. Dancing is mostly about attitude, so you want to feel confident! Shoes with thin, smooth soles and short heels are great for dancing. Open-toed shoes, flip-flops, and running shoes aren't recommended.

What to bring: Bring a bottle of water and an open mind!

How much it will cost: The price will vary depending on the following factors.

- Group lessons, or a private instructor
- One session, or a six-week class
- The studio—Most of the well-known ballroom studios offer the first lesson for free! But be aware, the instructor is also a trained salesperson who would like nothing more than to have you back every week!

Communicate: Your dance instructor is there to create a relaxing, non-judgmental, enjoyable environment for you to learn in. If you have a question, if you need to have something repeated, or if you feel any physical discomfort during the lesson, say something!

Don't be shy! Ballroom dancing is a social form of dance! You may dance with your instructor, and in a group setting, you might be asked to trade partners and temporarily dance with someone new. It is all part of the experience, and that's how you get better at leading or following.

Here are some great couples dances you might want to consider learning, depending on your skill level, physical fitness, and sense of adventure:

- Salsa
- Waltz
- Tango
- Foxtrot
- Hustle
- East/West Coast Swing
- Shag
- Line dances

"True love is when you're still dancing, long after the music stops."

128 Hey, Good Lookin'! What's Cookin'?

Are you bored with the typical dinner date? Taking an evening cooking class together is a fun alternative. And, even better, there's no preparation or clean up, you don't have to design the menu, and you'll get to try something new without the risk failure! Are you ready to get cooking?

Search local cooking schools online, and you'll be surprised at how easy this date is to organize.

What to Expect

Register in advance (usually online) and expect to pay approximately $50 per person. But before you balk at the expense, remember that this is your meal and your activity for the night. (And you don't have to tip the waiter!)

What You Will Cook

During a two-hour class you can expect to whip up three to four tasty dishes. You can look at the schedule to choose whether you want to try Thai, Italian, Mexican, sushi, and so on. Do you need a gluten-free evening? Are you a vegan? Just check the schedule, and you'll find a meal to suit your taste and dietary needs.

Who You Will Be Cooking With

You class will have four to six other students with a trained chef at the helm.

As you can hopefully see, this date doesn't require any cooking skills or experience. It's a fun and (almost) foolproof process, so no worries! Your primary focus should be on having a great time together. Enjoy the chance to see your partner in a new light and learn something new together—and you'll be able to dine on your creations at the end of the class.

129 Sign-Language Class

Look to a community college, community center, social services, or a library to learn this useful skill. Some basic classes might be offered for free through a library or church group, while more extensive training will have a fee. Why should you learn to sign?

- You can communicate with your hearing-impaired friends, neighbors, coworkers, etc. Hearing loss is much more common than you might think.
- You will better meet your young child's needs. Babies can learn simple signs long before they are ready to speak.
- People find it to be fascinating, beautiful, unique, graceful, and expressive.
- Learning a second language enriches and enhances your cognitive processes: higher abstract and creative thinking, better problem solving, greater cognitive flexibility, and better listening skills.
- Finger spelling will help you become a better speller!
- You can communicate with each other silently or have a private talk in public (at your own risk, of course!). You can even talk conveniently in sign language with your mouth full or talk from a distance without shouting.

What marriage wouldn't benefit from an extra way to communicate? And once you learn this new form of communication, you will also gain a new way to serve your community together!

130 LEARN TO PLAY THE UKULELE

This remarkable instrument is perfect for you, whether you're a seasoned musician or can barely tap your foot in rhythm. Why should you learn the ukulele?

- It's inexpensive! A ukulele will cost anywhere from $25 up, depending on the size, quality, and type.
- It's easy to learn! There are only four strings on a ukulele, and they are easier to press and hold down than guitar strings, so you could be playing songs after one thirty-minute lesson!
- It's small and easy to carry! Just toss it in your backpack for your romantic hike or carry it in your car for those long-distance sing-alongs. It's much more maneuverable than a guitar!
- It's adaptable! Almost any song can be played on the ukulele with a few simple chords.
- It's fun! Playing or listening to the ukulele will make you smile.

Do a little research about which type to purchase (soprano, concert, tenor, or baritone) and watch some videos, and you'll be an expert before you know it!

131 Improv Class

So you think you can act? Why not try taking a comedy improv class together? These classes are usually inexpensive (around $25 per person, per class) and last a couple of hours. "Actors" are encouraged to test their skills in creating characters on the spot through short-form comedy improv. What a great way to get out of your dating rut and laugh together. Check with your city or town arts council to find a class near you.

132 Home Improvement

Did you know that your local home-improvement store probably offers do-it-yourself classes for free? You can sign up together to learn anything from installing a toilet, laying floor tile, or installing a ceiling fan to building small accessories for your home. If home improvement of any kind is on your to-do list, don't miss a chance to nurture your relationship by learning these skills together.

133 Jewelry-Making Class

There are some pretty great reasons to learn how to make jewelry. And taking a class together makes the value of this new skill even greater!

In a basic beading class, you will usually learn how to make a necklace, bracelet, or earrings. (If you aren't interested beading, try wire wrapping, pendant wrapping, or silk knotting pearls, to suggest a few.) This will only cost you around $25–$30 per person, including materials. There is usually a "bead budget" included in the price, which allows you to choose your own colors and styles so your creation will be uniquely YOU. (You can choose beads that are more expensive if you want to pay the difference). There will be an instructor to walk you through the technical aspects of attaching clasps, hooks, and so on, and to give you as much creative advice as you need.

Learning to make jewelry together has many advantages.

- You always have a unique and personalized gift to give.
- You always have jewelry to match your outfit.
- If you learn the basics, you can usually repair broken jewelry as well.

Even if you are not the type to wear a lot of jewelry, you can use this opportunity to make a present for a special family member or friend. A daughter, a mother, or a grandmother will appreciate that you took time to create a meaningful gift together. And if you really like it, you can come back and take a more advanced class later!

134 POTTERY CLASS

A one-time pottery class is a great way to learn the fundamentals from an instructor while you have fun playing with clay on the wheel. You'll make something simple the first time, and then you will get to pick out a glaze to give your creation that final finishing touch. Depending on your studio's policy, your piece will be fired and ready to pick up in three to four weeks.

Usually all materials are included in your registration fee, and the average class time is 60–90 minutes. You'll be with a group (probably no larger than ten people) and it will cost you $25–$35, depending on your area. Call around and check reviews online to choose the class that you want to take, and then register in advance.

Show up with your long hair tied back, trimmed fingernails, and no jewelry on your hands, and be prepared to get a little dirty. In a clean way, of course!

135 SELF-RELIANCE / FINANCIAL-LITERACY CLASS

It's a widely known fact that one of the top reasons for divorce in this country is finance related; differences in money-management styles between two partners can ruin a marriage. In fact, living in poverty is incredibly stressful, and financial stressors can lead to fighting. There is no need to wait until you are struggling to confront this issue together. And if you are already concerned about finances or having trouble providing for the needs of your family, you and your sweetheart should get yourselves enrolled in a financial-literacy class—yesterday.

Where can we find a class to take? Start with your church! Financial health and spiritual health are tied directly together, and more often church leaders these days are recognizing this. Also try public libraries and community colleges.

How can we pay for a class if we are already in trouble financially? Many times these classes are free or on a sliding scale based on income. Don't assume you can't afford it—this could be the best financial decision you've made in a long time.

How will talking about money problems strengthen our marriage? Because you are going to a class, you won't just be talking about how poor you are. You'll be discussing ways to solve your financial issues. You will be honest about your goals and your fears, possibly for the first time, and you'll see that others are facing the same worries. Ultimately, you'll set goals, you'll learn each other's spending and saving styles, and you will grow closer as a couple.

136 PAINT THE TOWN

Paint nights are the newest global craze among the young and old alike! Do-it-yourself painting franchises are popping up everywhere. There are also painting events open to the public and hosted by local clubs and restaurants. This date might be a tiny bit pricey (around $30–$50 per person), but if you have a special occasion or something to celebrate, go ahead and take the plunge. Not only with you leave with great memories and a new skill, but you'll also bring home some new artwork to hang in your home!

What to Expect

- Reservations are made ahead of time, usually online, where you can see a picture of the image you will be recreating in your class.
- A professional instructor will lead you in a step-by-step process of creating a work of art on your own canvas.
- Classes that are held specifically for couples will offer the opportunity to create a diptych (artwork consisting of two painted panels, which are hung side by side to create one larger image), so you don't have to bring home two versions of the same painting.
- You can often bring your own drinks and snacks (confirm ahead of time at your location).
- Smocks will be provided at the event, but it's likely that you'll get some paint on your clothing or shoes, so dress appropriately.

After you've attended one of these painting parties, it'll be easy to see why these events have become hugely popular! They make great dates for couples, precisely because they provide an activity to do together without the pressure of being completely one-on-one. Best of all, they'll give you a peek into your partner's creative side!

Ready, set, CREATE!

137 SELF-DEFENSE CLASS

Lets face it—the world we live in is not always the safest place, and that can be a little scary. A good way to feel confident and secure might be to learn strategies and techniques to defend yourself. Taking a self-defense class together will help you work as a team in the event that the unspeakable happens.

Look to martial arts schools and YMCAs if you don't mind paying for a defense training course, but you might find a free class by checking with your local fire station, police station, college campus, or parks and recreation department. You can even learn from home by finding online courses or YouTube videos that teach basic techniques.

'TIS THE SEASON

Holidays throughout the year provide many opportunities for unique dates and romantic traditions.

138 HOLIDAY CONCERT

If you're looking for a special evening out with your sweetie this holiday season, attend a holiday concert together! Aside from Valentine's Day, Christmas is the most romantic holiday for most couples, and it gives you a great excuse to pull out that Christmas sweater, and to get a little bit nostalgic.

What is your style? Do you love classical music? If so, look for concerts featuring symphonies such as Tchaikovsky's famous "Waltz of the Flowers" from *The Nutcracker*, Bach's joyous "Christmas Oratorio," or Franz Lizst's charming "Christmas Tree Suite." Do you prefer traditional Christmas carols? Look for festive carol concerts, sing-alongs, or modern choirs. Are you looking for a more religious setting for the music? Go to a church or cathedral choir performance.

Reserve spaces early because these feel-good concerts fill up fast during the holidays! If your spouse is comfortable with it, dress up. Many people will be dressed to the nines, and, while you might not need to go that far, a holiday concert is the perfect opportunity for a little extra effort and that festive attire that you seem to only wear once a year.

"It'll nearly be like a picture print
By Currier and Ives
These wonderful things are the things
We remember all through our lives!"

(Leroy Anderson and Mitchell Parish, "Sleigh Ride," 1948)

139 SECRET SANTA

There is truly nothing that brings the joy of the season like a super-secret service project for someone who might not otherwise be feeling the spirit of Christmas. Who do you know that could use a little extra Christmas cheer?

Do you know of a family in need? What about a recent widow or widower who might be feeling alone this year? Do you have a friend who just went through a divorce? What about your local fire station that is staffed with volunteers on Christmas? What about your mail carrier or package delivery person who is working late and away from family? A policeman? A doctor or nurse?

Once you've chosen a person or group that you'd like to serve, you are already feeling the love, and that feeling will permeate your relationship with your spouse as well!

What would Santa do now? Think of your budget and what you have time to accomplish. Caution: Do not allow this act of service to bring you, your spouse, or your family any added holiday stress! Whatever you choose to do, remember that it's the act of love and kindness that counts. Maybe you can provide gifts for the whole family down the street that is struggling financially. Good for you! Or maybe you can bake a plate of homemade cookies and deliver them to the fire station on Christmas Eve. You can leave a little gift card for the mail carrier just to let them know that you notice their hard work or show up to sing Christmas carols at the door of a widow. The love you show will be the love you feel between the two of you, and you will look forward to this date next year! Below are some ideas listed based on potential price.

Low-Budget Service Ideas ($)

- Bake cookies to deliver to the fire station.
- Leave a gift card for the mail carrier.
- Sing Christmas carols at the door or a widow.
- Deliver hand-made Christmas ornaments to a senior center.
- Invite an elderly couple, a newly wed couple, or a couple that's far from home over for a Christmas movie night.

Mid-Budget Service Ideas ($$)

- Make dinner for a family that is going through a hard time.
- Check with a service organization that gathers Christmas gifts for needy children in your area. They'll usually provide you with a child's age, gender, and clothing sizes. Shop together for a gift.

High-Budget Service Ideas ($$$)

- Provide gifts for a family that is struggling financially.
- Take a family to see *The Nutcracker*.

140 GINGERBREAD HOUSES: FROM A FIXER UPPER TO A SHOWPLACE!

This Christmas tradition makes a great double or triple date—the more the merrier! A crackling fireplace and festive music will add to the atmosphere when your guests begin to arrive with their gingerbread house kit in tow, ready to put their creativity to the test.

Each couple will need their own workspace, where they will work together to design an HGTV-show-worthy house design, using only the kit they came with. You may wish to provide each couple with a blank "blueprint" (graph paper) to plan their renovations. Trading supplies with other "builders" and "designers" is perfectly acceptable, as extensive remodeling may be necessary.

Have fun working in teams, and when everyone is done, each couple should have a "reveal," as if they were home remodeling show hosts.

If you'd like to reward the champions, have prizes on hand for the best gingerbread home—and for those who may lack in skill but had the best "team effort."

141 CHRISTMAS LIGHTS WITH MUSIC AND HOT CHOCOLATE

What could be more romantic than twinkling lights, Christmas music, and hot chocolate? This date is truly as easy as 1-2-3, and it's just what you need to get into that festive holiday spirit. It might even be a great way to decompress after an evening shopping trip.

1. Swing by a coffee shop and pick up a large cup of hot chocolate. Ask them to add peppermint for a holiday twist!
2. Find that radio station that plays Christmas music for two solid months, or choose your own favorites with a music app on your phone.
3. Take a drive through *that* neighborhood—the one that keeps the power company in business for the holidays with millions of lights. Every town has one!
4. Hold hands and drive slowly. Sip your hot chocolate, and soak in the season and the romance!

142 FIND AND DECORATE A CHRISTMAS TREE

In many families, searching for the perfect Christmas tree involves the children and sometimes even the family pet! If your family enjoys this holiday tradition, hold onto it as long as the kids are young and cooperative! But what if you don't have children yet or all of your little turtledoves have left the nest?

Turn the hunt for the perfect tree into a new date tradition! Do you pick up a tree from the farmer who has set up shop down on the corner? Do you hike up a mountain, axe in hand, and drag your spoils all the way home? Or, like more and more of us, does finding your tree involve more of a climb up the attic stairs with a flashlight and a duster in hand? However you find your Christmas tree, the experience will mean so much more if it's shared by the one you love the most. Put on some romantic holiday music, share some yummy treats, and decorate your tree together for the perfect stay-at-home date!

143 CHRISTMAS CAROLING (GROUP)

Some holiday traditions never go out of style, and Christmas caroling is one of them! Unless you and your spouse are super confident in your singing voices, you might want to invite another couple or two to come along and add some volume. Dress for the season, both warm and festive, and have a hot cup of cocoa before your little group takes to the streets.

Where to Go

Visit friends who would enjoy your surprise. Visit the elderly who may need a little more Christmas cheer. Don't forget to visit the Ebenezer Scrooge who lives down the street. Your music and enthusiasm would be especially appreciated in a nursing home or assisted living facility. You could stroll down the halls as you sing familiar carols, or if someone in your group plays the piano, you could all gather around and turn it into a sing-along!

Wherever you decide to go, remember that 'tis the season for fresh-baked cookies as well as holiday carols. And if your singing is not so great, you can leave them with a treat to make up for it!

144 Thrills and Roller-Coaster Hills

If you have an amusement park or theme park nearby, you have an absolutely amazing date just waiting to happen. A theme park can mean tons of adult fun with a hearty splash of happy childhood nostalgia thrown in as well. The sheer number of activities, from rides to roller-coasters to games and shows, means that you don't have an opportunity to get bored. Even if you have to stand in line for a while, take the opportunity to chat or to people-watch. You won't have any danger of running out of things to talk about.

The Plan

- Learn all you can about the park in advance. Research the busiest seasons and time of day, and learn the park policies (parking, bringing food in, carrying backpacks, etc.).
- Know the park hours for the day you'll be going, and check the weather. A rainy day can ruin your date just as much as a 100-degree day can. Many parks even have apps that include up-to-date park information and even current wait times.
- Buy tickets online in advance to save time standing in line. This is also a good way to save money if online coupons are available. Some smaller theme parks might even have less-expensive evening hours and offer discounts to locals in the off-season.

What to Bring

Bring only the absolute essentials into the park—keep in mind that you have to carry everything with you!

- Personal items such as medications, sunscreen, lip balm, and hand sanitizer.
- Hat and sunglasses
- Ziplock bag (to put your cell phone in on the water rides)
- Poncho (to stay dry on water rides and in a sudden shower)
- Refillable water bottle
- Cash

What to Wear

Dress for the weather, of course, but most importantly, *wear good shoes*. Don't let this adventure with your sweetie be ruined by blisters and aching knees! Flip-flops and other open-toed shoes may not be the best for roller-coasters and lots of walking.

Important Tips

Remember where you parked! It's a good idea to take a picture of your parking spot location so you don't forget it after a long day at the park! You're going to be way too tired to wander around the parking lot at the end of the day.

Take time to rest your feet and enjoy the view! Watching a show or a parade is a great way to enjoy the park while getting off your feet!

Leave the games and souvenirs for the end! Remember that you'll have to carry around whatever you get, and your mad skills at the ring toss might just win you win that giant stuffed teddy bear!

145 HALLOWEEN-THEMED AMUSEMENT PARK DATES

If you and your sweetie are looking to quench your thirst for all things spooky, theme parks across the nation have taken their Halloween experiences to the next level! Look online for theme parks nearby, and you can be sure they are dressing the place up for Halloween. With professional makeup artists and costume designers, second-to-none light shows, and ghoulish sound effects, a haunted amusement park date is not the date to bring young children along for. As a matter of fact, you might find yourself running for the car before your evening is through! (Pricing and hours are sometimes adjusted for the season, so be sure to do your homework!)

146 CHRISTMAS-THEMED AMUSEMENT PARK DATES

When most people think of dates around Christmastime, theme parks probably don't come to mind. But if the weather in your area is survivable and you need to take a break from the stress that seems to follow the holidays around like a lost reindeer, this could be just what you and your partner need. Your favorite amusement park will not disappoint with festive decorations, twinkling lights, and the music of the season. This festive date will lift your Christmas spirits and remind you of the joy that comes from the season. You might even find Santa hanging around, ready to jot down your wish list! (Pricing and hours are sometimes adjusted for the season, so be sure to do your homework!)

147 The Great Pumpkin Contest

Ahh, autumn . . . That time of year when most of the country is pulling out their sweaters and putting away their flip flops, putting away the ice cream and warming up the hot chocolate and cider! Everywhere you turn, there is a sea of beautiful orange pumpkins for sale. Sounds like it might be time to issue a playful date-night challenge!

Pumpkin patches bring out the Charlie Brown in all of us as we search for the perfect gourd to grace our front stoop for the next month or so. This fruit (or vegetable—botanists define it as both!) comes in many shapes, sizes, colors, and even patterns. They range from the size of a softball to the I'm-going-to-need-a-truck-to-get-that-one-home size. Most of us look for a giant pumpkin to turn into our jack-o-lantern for Halloween, but the smaller ones are fun too, and they only cost a few dollars each.

Let the Games Begin!

So are you ready to challenge your sweetie to a little creative competition? How about a pumpkin-decorating contest?

Your date will start at the pumpkin patch in search of candidates for the title of Great Pumpkin. Decide together on your plan. Are you going to decorate one large pumpkin each, or a couple of small ones? Once you've decided, go ahead and pick out whatever your budget will allow.

(Prices will vary greatly, depending on when you buy your pumpkin and what part of the country you are in.)

How Are You Going to Decorate?

Traditional carving? Permanent markers? (Don't forget the metallic kind!) Paint? (Use acrylic with a spray sealant for weatherproofing.) Ribbons, fabric, and glue?

Not the creative type? If you search the term "pumpkin decorating ideas" on the internet, you'll come up with more ideas than you know what to do with!

After you have picked your pumpkin from the pumpkin patch and shown off your artistic pizzazz, it's time for the judging! Let the kids (or grandchildren) be the judges and bestow the Great Pumpkin award to the winner.

And for the Grand Prize, the Winner Receives . . .

50 kisses! (Chocolate or otherwise—you decide.) And top placement by the front door, of course! Happy decorating!

148 LOST IN YOUR . . . EARS?

Going through a corn maze together is something that can become a tradition each year. Not only does it give you time to talk with each other, but you're also solving a problem together. Depending on your preference, this can be a nice, leisurely autumn stroll that gives you an opportunity to admire the beautiful fall colors—very relaxing and romantic. Or if you or your spouse are into the chills and thrills of the season, it can be a creepy nighttime trail filled with jump scares and plenty of chances to hold on to each other tightly. Try both options. Two completely different experiences in the same location gives you more opportunities to hang out and have fun together.

149 PLAYING CUPID

When February rolls around, we generally look forward to a special card, a romantic night out, or a gift from our sweetheart. Valentine's Day is all about making certain that your special someone knows how truly cherished they are, and as consumers, we spare no expense in doing so. Americans spend literally *billions* of dollars on Valentine's Day merchandise each year.

So what can you do to take out some of the materialism of the holiday and add more love? Play Cupid!

Think of three people that you know are spending this romantic night alone. Maybe they are single, widowed, or have a spouse who is far away (traveling on business, in the armed forces, etc.). Once you've picked your three friends, decide how you want to approach the next step.

Artsy-Crafty

Travel back in time to your elementary school days, when you used construction paper, lace, and glue to make cards. Cut out hearts and use stickers and markers to make a special card for your friends. Tell them that they are loved and that you are thinking of them. Sign the card "Your Valentines," and add your names.

Not So Artsy-Crafty

Go to a gift shop or card store that has a wide selection of Valentines. Take the time to read and pick out special cards for each one of your friends. Have a little fun reading cards to each other as well! Once you've chosen your favorites and purchased them, write special notes and sign "Your Valentines," and add your names.

A Little Extra

Pick up a box of chocolates for each friend if you'd like to add a bit more sweetness to your gift. (Don't forget to grab some candy for yourselves to enjoy in the car as you drive from house to house!) If you really want to brighten someone's day, add a bouquet of flowers!

The rest of the plan is simple. Hop in the car, play some love songs, and start making your deliveries. Since you are dropping by unexpectedly, don't plan to spend a lot of time visiting. A few minutes at each stop is enough time to "play Cupid" by spreading a little love to those who need it.

Spending an evening focused on others who are without their special Valentine will remind you to cherish yours.

150 I've Got My Love to Keep Me Warm

Who says picnics are only for the summer? A winter picnic has its advantages! You don't need to bring a cooler, you won't be pestered by bugs, and being wrapped up in a blanket with your soul mate while snow falls all around is very, very romantic. Just remember to wear extra socks to make that impromptu winter stroll a little more comfortable.

ABOUT THE AUTHORS

Nick and Mendy Greenwood grew up in different North Carolina cities and met at the beach right after high school graduation. They were married in February of 1991. Together, they worked toward Nick's BFA from East Carolina University, and starting in 1995, they had four beautiful daughters. In twenty-seven years of marriage, they have moved twelve times, faced numerous health challenges, career changes, broken-down cars, sparse cupboards, teenage angst, mood swings, ups, downs, highs, lows, and STILL, their favorite place to be is anywhere—together. Their secret to a long and happy marriage is this: Hold hands, say please and thank you, and never stop dating.

Scan to visit

www.nickgreenwood.net